A Primer of Kleinian Therapy

Irving Solomon, Ph.D.

JASON ARONSON INC.
Northvale, New Jersey
London

This book was set in 11-point English Times by TechType of Upper Saddle River, New Jersey, and printed and bound by Haddon Craftsmen of Scranton, Pennsylvania.

Library of Congress Cataloging-in-Publication Data

Solomon, Irving.
    A primer of Kleinian therapy / by Irving Solomon.
      p. cm.
    Includes bibliographical references and index.
    ISBN 1-56821-391-3
    1. Klein, Melanie. 2. Psychodynamic psychotherapy. I. Title.
    [DNLM: 1. Klein, Melanie. 2. Psychoanalytic Therapy. WM 460.6
  S689p 1995]
    RC438.6.K58S65   1995
    616.89'17 – dc20
    DNLM/DLC
    for Library of Congress   94-36578

Manufactured in the United States of America. Jason Aronson Inc. offers books and cassettes. For information and catalog write to Jason Aronson Inc., 230 Livingston Street, Northvale, New Jersey 07647.

THE LIBRARY OF OBJECT RELATIONS

A SERIES OF BOOKS EDITED BY
DAVID E. SCHARFF AND JILL SAVEGE SCHARFF

Object relations theories of human interaction and development provide an expanding, increasingly useful body of theory for the understanding of individual development and pathology, for generating theories of human interaction, and for offering new avenues of treatment. They apply across the realms of human experience from the internal world of the individual to the human community, and from the clinical situation to everyday life. They inform clinical technique in every format from individual psychoanalysis and psychotherapy, through group therapy, to couple and family therapy.

The Library of Object Relations aims to introduce works that approach psychodynamic theory and therapy from an object relations point of view. It includes works from established and new writers who employ diverse aspects of British, American, and international object relations theory in helping individuals, families, couples, and groups. It features books that stress integration of psychoanalytic approaches with marital, family, and group therapy, as well as those centered on individual psychotherapy and psychoanalysis.

Refinding the Object and
Reclaiming the Self
David E. Scharff

Scharff Notes: A Primer of
Object Relations Therapy
*Jill Savege Scharff and
David E. Scharff*

Object Relations Couple
Therapy
*David E. Scharff and
Jill Savege Scharff*

Object Relations Family
Therapy
*David E. Scharff and
Jill Savege Scharff*

Projective and Introjective
Identification and the Use
of the Therapist's Self
Jill Savege Scharff

Foundations of Object
Relations Family Therapy
Jill Savege Scharff, Editor

For my grandchildren
Daniel, Rebecca, and Jacklyn

Contents

Acknowledgments

A great many people helped me in the preparation of this book. Dr. Stephen Block graciously allowed me to use a number of his cases to illustrate important aspects of the Kleinian model and technique. Dr. David Scharff kindly read the manuscript and made many useful suggestions. Dr. Edward Tobe suggested an important sequence of presentation, and Judy Cohen, editor at Jason Aronson, contributed a number of valuable ideas, considerably strengthening the manuscript stylistically.

As usual, my colleagues and friends, Drs. Edward Penzer, Bernice Barber, and Dale Mendell offered moral support and emotional sustenance.

Finally, I would like to thank my wife, Sandra, for her assistance and encouragement while I was working on the primer.

Introduction

EVERY MODEL OF THERAPY
HAS ITS OWN SPECIFIC TERMS,
ITS OWN LANGUAGE. HOW DO
YOU DEFINE THE CENTRAL
IDEAS OF KLEINIAN THEORY
AND TECHNIQUE?

Phantasy: Phantasy spelled with a "ph" to distinguish it
from *fantasy*, a conscious daydream, is a specific, complex
unconscious constellation of libido, aggression, defenses,

anxieties, self, and internal objects as they interact affectively in the patient's inner world.

Paranoid-schizoid position: The first three months of the infant's life, according to Melanie Klein (1946), are characterized by a complexity of persecutory anxieties, threats, fears of annihilation, splitting of the ego and of the self into good and bad, projective identification and defenses such as omnipotence, idealization, and denial against paranoid anxieties. During this time frame, healthy splitting leads to integration, whereas pathological splitting leads to fragmentation.

Depressive position: The depressive position occurs approximately within the second quarter of the first year of the infant's life. The infant begins to recognize that part-objects are really whole objects; the same object that is hated is also loved; projective identification and splitting are diminished; the infant feels guilt, concern, and a desire to repair the damaged object. The anxiety caused by damage to the object is depressive anxiety.

The Oedipus complex is dependent on the successful resolution of the depressive position; this is the acceptance of the separate relationship of the primary object to another object. Envy is diminished, ego integration is increased, and, with the greater tolerance of ambivalence, reality testing is strengthened.

Manic defenses: To ward off the anxiety of the depressive position, the infant may develop manic defenses. The manic defenses refer to denial, omnipotence, disparagement, triumph, excessive control, and idealization. There may be an attempt to repair the injured external object, but the repair is forced, nongenuine and ultimately spoiling.

Projective identification: This refers to the patient's forcing aspects of his internal world, (e.g., part- and whole objects, anxieties, self, affects, defenses) into the analyst's mentation. The purpose of projective identification can vary, for example, communication, control, safeguarding the good self and/or good objects from the bad, getting rid of the bad internal objects, and empathy.

There is as yet no adequate explanation of how projective identification occurs other than the possibility that there may be some subtle, nonverbal conditioning and/or nudging by the patient — or the infant in the patient — into the analyst as "mother" or "father."

Projective identification is a Kleinian concept that is used very frequently to clarify the back-and-forth shifts of transference–countertransference and defenses against projective identification through monitoring of the therapist's inner world within the session. Most often, the analyst catches and understands a patient's projective identifications by experiencing his own fantasies, anxieties, and bodily tensions. Projective identifications, of course, do occur outside the treatment room as well.

Introjection: This is the process of first internalizing a part-object, the mother's good, nourishing, idealized breast, the basis of ego-strength. Taking the mother in, the infant absorbs her acceptance, tolerance, and capacity to reduce stress. This introjection is at the heart of an adult's acceptance of him- or herself. The taking in of a "bad" breast, or a mother who provides a bad experience of feeding, may lead to a nameless dread and a lifelong conviction of being a worthless human being.

If the patient puts bad projective identification into the therapist (e.g., anger through introjection), the patient then may take back the bad and experience self-hatred, a depressive anxiety, and guilt.

In essence, through introjection, the individual creates a complex inner world filled with good, bad, and idealized internal objects affectively relating to each other, the self, and the external world. Introjection is intensified during the depressive position.

Splitting: One of the earliest defenses (occurring during the paranoid-schizoid position), it exists to separate the good from the bad experiences, to safeguard the good primary internal objects (i.e., the parental figure or part-object breast, nipple, or penis) from danger. Splitting also refers to the splitting of the ego as well as of the internal and external object.

Splitting into good and bad can help the infant organize and integrate chaotic experiences. Ego integration leads to an increased capacity to tolerate ambivalence.

Envy: In Klein's book *Envy and Gratitude* (1957), she elaborated and clarified a most significant affect, self-and-object relationship, which up until then had not been given enough consideration.

Envy differs from jealousy in that envy wants to destroy what the other person has. Jealousy covets what the other has but consents to allow him or her to have it. Envy is in the service of hatred and spoiling. Greed is associated with envy in that the envious individual is more concerned with taking away what the other possesses than with actively obtaining it for him- or herself. Envy causes carping, criticality, devaluing, ruthlessness, compulsive ambition, sarcasm, mockery. The envious person cannot enjoy the good he or she has because there is always the projected paranoid anxiety that the other, out of envy, will steal the good from him or her. Excessive envy impairs the capacity to take in information and interpretations, since the giver's capacity to inform or interpret is a "good," perhaps an idealized "good" that the envious individual wants for him- or herself, wants to take away, wants to destroy. Excessive envy and defenses against it originate during the paranoid-schizoid position as a consequence of infantile bad experiences outweighing good experiences. Consequently, the infant's subsequent depressive position tenure (i.e., a greater tolerance for ambivalent feelings) does not soften the affect of envy enough.

Container/contained: Bion (1962) proposed the concept of *container* as a useful view of the analyst's maternal mental state of holding, the emotionally safe sanctuary created during the session.

The infant in the patient is the *contained*, held comfortably by the analyst's mental state of reverie, cognitively and affectively carried by the analyst just as a mother gazing upon her crying baby takes in emotionally the baby's tension and, in return, offers calming, soothing relief. The analyst is aware of the patient's projections of distress into him or her and defines the projections through capable interpretations; thus the therapist gives the patient what he or she ultimately always needs: integration replacing chaos.

WHAT IS KLEINIAN PSYCHOTHERAPY?

Kleinian therapy is the application of Melanie Klein's theory and the contributions of her colleagues and students to once- or twice-per-week psychotherapy.

Kleinian theory and technique are already being applied to psychoanalysis but they have not been systematically discussed as an application to once- or twice-per-week therapy. Ask any practicing therapist and you will discover that almost 90 percent of his or her practice consists of patients seen once or twice per week.

Based on the literature, my own clinical experience, and that of my supervisees, it is evident that the Kleinian model offers valuable, unique insights into difficult therapy problems and impasses. The Kleinian model sharpens the therapist's recognition of transference–countertransference reactions, subtle dynamics, and, in general, the patient's phantasy world. This understanding is especially vital as once-per-week therapy offers the therapist a narrow window of opportunity to translate insights into meaningful growth.

CAN YOU PROVIDE SOME PERSONAL INFORMATION ABOUT MELANIE KLEIN?

Melanie Klein (née Reizes) was born in Vienna in 1882, the daughter of a poor Jewish doctor. She died in London in 1968.

Only now are her ideas becoming more recognized as powerful contributions to psychoanalytic therapy. Open any recent psychoanalytic journal or book and you will find the ideas of projective identification, splitting, reparation, the paranoid-schizoid position, the depressive position, and container, fundamental concepts originated by Klein and her adherents.

While Melanie Klein's life was productive and at times joyful, it was also filled with many losses and profound tragedies. Her beloved sister, Sidonie, four years her senior, died at 8. Her adored older brother, Emanuel, died under mysterious circumstances when Melanie was 20, and her oldest son, Hans, died of a fall from a mountain path. She endured other losses as well. Karl Abraham, her analyst and supporter, died at an early age. For many years estranged from her husband, Arthur, she divorced him in 1924. Melitta, her daughter, who was also a psychoanalyst, bitterly quarreled with Melanie, sided with Anna Freud's adherents, and lost no opportunity to attack her mother's work virulently at professional meetings. Melanie had also to face the formidable opposition of Anna Freud herself, daughter of the venerated founder of psychoanalysis, Sigmund Freud. Anna Freud was truly an extension of her father, having been his patient, a colleague, a confidante, and ultimately his devoted nurse during his declining years. Finally, Klein's lover, Chezkel Zvi Kloetzel, a journalist, ended their affair and moved to Palestine in 1923.

Melanie Klein, like Anna Freud, was not a physician. Nonetheless, the early analysts, for example Ferenczi, Abraham, and Jones, to their great credit, encouraged and accepted Klein's status as a lay analyst. Her first analyzed work with very young children convinced her that the formation of the superego began a lot earlier than Freud had observed. Klein inferred from her observations of her child patients that they possessed a complex phantasy world and that it was vital to interpret anxiety and other aspects of this world to the patient.

Her book, *The Psychoanalysis of Children*, published in 1932, gave Klein the opportunity to present more fully in clinical detail the theory and technique basic to her future ideas, the paranoid-schizoid and depressive positions. She laid out the complex inner world of the very young infant and child that is derived from introjection of and projection into external objects. She postulated, based on clinical intuitions and observations, the existence of immense sadistic impulses causing psychotic anxieties that could, with regard to development, be either productive or pathological. She described the formation (transformation of the death instinct) of the early stages of the superego. She explicitly talked about the life and death instincts, antecedents of her major theoretical and clinical ideas, the paranoid-schizoid and depressive positions. Anxiety was caused by the death instinct's danger to the self.

Her work *Love, Guilt and Reparation*, written with Joan Riviere and appearing in 1937, dealt with hate, guilt, aggression, love, and reparation. According to Klein, reparation and concern originated from infancy on, a view she later modified. Her final conclusion in subsequent writings was that reparation does not appear in the paranoid-schizoid position but in the more integrated depressive organization.

Klein's last theoretical contribution, *Envy and Gratitude*, published in 1957, elaborated extensively on the concept in book's title. The feeding breast is the first object of envy and gratitude. Klein demonstrated the analysis of splitting and the consequences of introjected objects fragmented by hate. She formulated the huge complex role that excessive envy and defenses against envy (e.g., splitting, idealization) play within the paranoid-schizoid position. She discussed the feeding breast as the source of creativity and how excessive envy destroys creativity. Her focus on envy shed light on a major therapeutic impasse, the *Negative Therapeutic Reaction* (NTR).

Her final major clinical work, and a wonderfully drawn case study, was *A Narrative of a Child Analysis*, published a year after her death in 1961. In it, Klein asserted that the Oedipus complex is linked to the beginning of the depressive position, as represented by Richard, the 10-year-old patient. It was a particularly outstanding example of her technique of reducing the child's psychotic anxieties through the exposure and increase of anxiety, subsequent interpretation, and working through of anxieties.

The founders of psychoanalytic schools of thought tended to evoke strong, varying, if not contradictory, reactions. Melanie Klein was no exception. Some analysts found her to be a clinical genius who was gentle, balanced, and respectful of individuality. Others saw her as dogmatic and dominating. However, she was experienced by a number of analysts who closely collaborated with her as a confident, warm, generous, lovable woman.

The only full-length biography of Melanie Klein is Phyllis Grosskurth's 1986 *Melanie Klein: Her World and her Work*. For further reading about Klein's life, work, and the subsequent contributions of her colleagues and followers, see the Suggested Reading section.

WHAT ARE THE POSSIBLE BARRIERS TO THE USE OF THE KLEINIAN MODEL?

For many mental health professionals, for example psychiatrists, psychologists, and social workers, the initial contact with Melanie Klein's ideas is, to say the least, jarring. They recoil from the Kleinian conviction that the infant below one year of age has an intricate inner world of phantasy that profoundly determines his subsequent adult behavior. To add to their dismay, Kleinian theory cannot be absolutely established with respect to clinical observations. How can we discover what an infant thinks and feels without the power of verbalization? Nonetheless, clinical experience with the Kleinian model suggests quite strongly that it is heuristically practical and valuable. There is a parallel here with the bumblebee. Aerodynamic engineers concluded from their study of the bee that it ought not to be able to fly. Of course it does, and quite well too. Kleinian theory and therapy equally fly quite well, as will be demonstrated in this book.

I urge the reader in his or her attitude toward Kleinian concepts to temporarily embrace the wisdom embodied in the following lines:

> To understand things we must have been once in them and then have come out of them; so that first there must be captivity and then deliverance, illusion followed by disillusion, enthusiasm by disappointment. He who is still under the spell, and he who has never felt the spell, are equally incompetent. We only know well what we have first believed, then judged. To understand we must be free, yet not have been always free. The same truth holds, whether it is a question of love, of art, of religion, or of patriotism. Sympathy is a first condition of criticism. [Amiel 1975, p. 78]

WHAT ROLE DOES PHANTASY PLAY IN THE KLEINIAN MODEL OF THERAPY?

Phantasy is the central core of the Kleinian understanding of the patient. Phantasy begins at birth and never stops. External events always dance with phantasies and their partnership eventuates in the reported experiences and nonverbal expressions of the patient.

Melanie Klein and her colleagues and students recognized that phantasy embodies object relations, anxieties, defenses, and, most importantly, two developmental constellations: the paranoid-schizoid position (in the first 3 or 4 months of life) and the depressive position (the last half of the first year of life). Each of the positions has its own array of parts of the self, internal objects, defenses, predominant affects, and capacity for insight.

The paranoid-schizoid position is characterized by frequent splitting off of parts of the self, external and internal objects, projective identification, persecutory fears, idealization of objects, a lack of responsibility, and a running away from inner reality and envy.

The depressive position carries with it a sense of responsibility and a willingness to stay with a realization of inner self, pain, and guilt.

The significance of the phantasy life of the patient as it plays itself out in terms of particular anxieties, internal parts of the self, objects, idealizations, and defenses is most clearly and powerfully expressed during immediate transference analysis. To grab hold of the patient's phantasies, we need to allow ourselves to experience how the patient is constantly forcing us into a certain role or compelling us to defend against a particular role.

CAN YOU GIVE AN EXAMPLE OF THE ROLE OF PHANTASY IN THERAPY?

Mrs. Vake, a 45-year-old teacher in a high school, had been involved with her married principal for over a year until she discovered that he also was involved sexually with another teacher. Furious, ashamed, and disillusioned, she ended the affair. In therapy, the patient wondered why she had become involved with a man who reported that he verbally abused his wife and subsequently betrayed her. What also confused her was her conviction that she respected and loved her husband, yet had become infatuated with the principal. When the principal left his girlfriend and wished to resume his relationship with the patient, she became alarmed that she was tempted to continue the affair.

Her background gives us some clues to her quandary: Her mother had always emphasized beauty. Her father was very good looking and was pursued by the mother. He apparently had held back his affection and appeared to have disdain for his wife. In actuality, Mrs. Vake's father was quite dependent on her mother.

To the patient, the principal was handsome, athletic, and generally much more exciting than her unathletic, plain-looking, "nerdy" husband. She bitterly attacked herself for being so influenced by what she termed "superficialities." Using the Kleinian model, what can we hypothesize at this juncture, realizing that our speculations are necessarily subject to ready modification should incompatible data emerge?

The patient's mother emphasized beauty, indicative of a part-object orientation. Kleinian theory points out that the fundamental formative processes of the infant's ego are introjection and projection. We would suspect, therefore, that through introjection of her mother's part-object emphasis on superficiality, for example, good looks, the patient would view herself and others on a part-object basis, an essential element of the paranoid-schizoid position.

The patient would compulsively be preoccupied with herself and another's perfect or imperfect beauty. Her mother had been scorned by her idealized father. Again, introjection would foster a striving for the perfectly attractive self or mate, another component of the paranoid-schizoid position. Excessive idealization, a given during the paranoid-schizoid position, ultimately leads to devaluation of the idealized object and/or self. We further suspect that the patient may ultimately devaluate both herself and an excessively valued part-object "beautiful" male. We would also anticipate that the patient might introject her father's dependency upon a devalued part-object, her mother. The patient would subsequently find herself conflicted between being the idealized one and devaluating the one who idealizes her, in this case, the principal. Since splitting and projective identification occur excessively during the paranoid-schizoid position, we would suppose that Mrs. Vake would split off her hated dependency and project it into her husband. He, in turn, would be denigrated. We would expect envy, another essential component of the paranoid-schizoid position, to be expressed toward her former lover for his good looks and ability to both attract and reject part-objects. The patient's self-attack for being influenced so much by "superficialities" (e.g., good looks) falls within the more advanced depressive position, because this is a yearning for a more total object- and total self-relationship and a greater capacity for appropriate concern for a significant object. Thus the patient regrets being influenced by "superficialities."

Pulling together many of the diverse dynamic elements in this instance from a Kleinian perspective, we would guess that the patient's central driving phantasy up until now may be as follows: an overall passionate pursuit of appearance over substance; the desire to control an introjected, part-object, idealized father projected into the external world in the form of the rejecting, "exciting" lover; an attempt to rid herself of the introjected, devalued mother projected into her "nerdy" husband; all the preceding factors in the service of preventing further fragmentation of the self, the main persecutory threat within the paranoid-schizoid position, since the idealized part-object inevitably becomes the chief persecutor of the self.

Therapy subsequently exposed Mrs. Vake's phantasy of introjecting her drab mother and having the idealized principal, as her father, pursue her. She had split off the introjected, unexciting mother and projected this maternal introject into her husband. She desperately wanted to be excited by her husband. Her guilty self-recriminations only served to repeat within her her father's attacks on her mother.

During a number of sessions following the initial interview, Mrs. Vake talked with disdain about her mother's obesity, her indifference to attractive clothing, her narrow dedication to cleaning, and her pursuit of her exciting but rejecting father. At the same time the patient said about herself, "I was a grossly overweight child up until adolescence and I did not care much about clothes." The patient's husband, too, was indifferent to clothes and overweight, making him an eminently suitable target for the patient's split-off projective identification of the maternal introject into him.

Even more ominously, the patient had also projected her scorned maternal introject into her daughter, an only child. Mrs. Vake, tears streaming down her face, proclaimed, "I hounded her. Kept after her, always on her to keep her weight down. She's very heavy but has a pretty face. We always bitterly fought over her weight. My husband would be furious with me for doing it but I kept at it. I deeply regret what I did to her now."

Her daughter was married and a very successful executive in a major, highly stressful corporation. During the early phase of therapy, the patient's daughter became deeply depressed and suicidal and had to be hospitalized. The patient severely blamed herself. "I did it. I nagged her about her appearance and never really appreciated all her great qualities. She's a good person, bright, kind, just like my husband."

It would seem that the patient, in defending against her own possible disintegration, a paranoid-schizoid threat, had rid herself of the bad, obese maternal introject by projecting it into her daughter. She could then freely express anger at the possibility that she fostered her daughter's move to a defiant, oppositional obesity along with perfectionistic, tormenting self-persecution and disintegration. The patient remembered how her father similarly verbally abused her: "You are just like your mother, fat and sloppy. How can you ever be happy looking the way you do!" She had found herself saying the same thing to her husband and daughter. She painfully added, "I destroyed my daughter. Look at her now. And I could destroy my marriage to a good man by running after my lover." She now was also feeling persecuted by the principal and by herself. She feverishly obsessed about the principal's ready sexual involvement with other women. Presumably to her he was having incredible, frequent sexual pleasures, the Kleinian version of the oedipal phantasy of the envied sexually combined parental couple.

In one session Mrs. Vake reported that she frequently imagined the principal "having sex with one of the younger pretty teachers who are so infatuated with him. Of course, he would grow tired of me. I'm 45 and they're 25. He's a great lover." And "As long as he *shtups* [has sex with] his wife," [she said enviously,] "she keeps quiet. I think about them jealously. I think that my husband is so much more of a better man than him. My husband has integrity and would never cheat on me. He's a family man, really hurting because of our daughter's illness."

Based on this understanding of the patient's phantasies we can formulate the following:

1. Help the patient become aware that she was projecting into the principal her exciting, rejecting father.
2. Help the patient recognize how she had introjected her unexciting mother and her self-hatred as a result.
3. Help the patient realize how much she has persecuted

herself through envy of the idealized principal and the
phantasy of the oedipal parental couple, that is, the
principal and his girlfriends. Last,

4. The most difficult therapeutic task, help the patient
   relocate and sense the substantive part of herself, that part
   concerned and responsible that was split off from her
   awareness and placed in others, that is, the therapist, her
   husband, and other family members.

inside/out

live in
* others*

By the therapist's repeatedly placing before the patient
her central phantasy, position-derivatives, projective identifications, envies, splitting, and resistances as they emerge
inside and outside of the session, she was helped to remain
more solidly in the depressive position. Thus she lived more
significantly for the substantive than for the superficial.

CAN YOU ILLUSTRATE THE VALUE OF THE KLEINIAN MODEL?

As I read Theodore J. Jacobs's courageous self-exposure of
his inner fantasy world paralleling the material of the patient,
Mr. V., in his paper "The Inner Experiences of the Analyst:
Their Contribution to the Analytic Process" (1993), I was
struck by how well the Kleinian model explains and antici-
pates the nature of the patient's central dynamics as framed
within one session. To substantiate this conclusion I shall
first give a brief summary of the flow of the hour, followed
by my Kleinian understanding of the session's central issues,
that is, the patient's inner phantasy world, resistances, transferences, countertransferences, and so on.

Jacobs carefully limits his account of the session to an
almost phenomenological description that intentionally

avoids any complex psychoanalytic analysis of the patient's dynamics. Jacobs's interpretations were obviously influenced by such basic, classical psychoanalytic concepts as transference, countertransference, resistance analysis, clarification of affects (e.g., envy), recognition of contradictions or conflicts, and the influence of defenses and early childhood traumas. It is, of course, quite possible that these same elements would ultimately be picked up by a classical Freudian. But I believe that the close fit between the Kleinian model and the emerging dynamics of the session is very impressive, a fine example of the value of Melanie Klein's enormous contribution to clinical understanding and technique.

The patient, Mr. V., 38, single, and an attorney, entered analysis for a number of reasons. He felt he had not attained enough professional success, was without friends, avoided his family, and was unable to make a commitment to marry a woman with whom he had lived for two years. In addition, he felt like a fake and had a fear of being discovered as inadequate. He had indifferent, self-involved parents and an indifferent older brother.

Jacobs describes Mr. V. as an invasive, intimidating man who would stand in the waiting room almost pressed against his office door before the session and furiously charge into the room when the door was opened. An interpretation to Mr. V. that this behavior represented his wish to take over Jacobs's office and life, while accepted by the patient, did not modify this behavior.

Having just moved into a newly decorated office, Jacobs shares at the beginning of his description of the session his expectation that the patient will typically be critical of the decor. As Jacobs anticipated Mr. V.'s disapproval, he himself felt increasingly uncomfortable and insecure about the appearance of his new office.

Mr. V. was always punctual and this trait of the patient

evoked in Jacobs an association to a tough sergeant and a writing teacher of his who had once confessed to a daily ritual he had to perform before beginning to write.

Mr. V. was dressed in expensive, elegant, English-style clothes in contrast to Jacobs, who noted that he himself dressed less fashionably and expensively. Jacobs thought that Mr. V., though Jewish, did not want to be considered Jewish, but Jacobs recognized that this thought of his might be motivated by envy and competitiveness. Jacobs realized at that moment that his transference to the patient might be based on a defense against aggression and rivalry; these feelings were similar to Jacobs's relationship with his own father and other male authority figures. Jacobs also remembered his father's volatile temper.

As Jacobs expected, Mr. V. began the session by scathingly and contemptuously criticizing the new office and its decor. Next, the patient denounced his older brother and a Mr. K., as wealthy, lucky idiots who were aspiring to undeserved elegance and status. The patient regretted having accepted a dinner invitation to Mr. K.'s home. Jacobs felt stomach tension as he recognized that Mr. V. was also indirectly being contemptuous of him. Jacobs picked up on the patient's concealed envy and called to Mr. V.'s attention that he himself had entertained the idea of moving to a more prestigious locale. Mr. V. was not fazed and merely affirmed through a bit of a rhyme that aspirants to new status were still impostors and deserved hanging. Jacobs pointed out the envy and anger at him, his older brother, and Mr. K. The patient brought up how envious he was as an adolescent of his older brother's sartorial splendor, and how his brother would not allow him to borrow his clothing. This same brother would make fun of the patient's physical appearance. Jacobs felt an angry identification with the patient at this moment and remembered childhood beatings that he and his

Jewish friends had undergone by Irish youth gangs. While Jacobs experienced his painful childhood memory, Mr. V. returned to his criticism of his older brother and Mr. K. for being phony, pious Jews.

As Mr. V. continued to criticize, Jacobs simultaneously had a series of memories as follows: an embarrassing incident involving his wearing poorly coordinated clothes, his grandparents' apartment with its *mezuzah*, a small metal symbol denoting a Jewish home, and the painted-over *mezuzah* on his new office door frame.

Jacobs asked the patient if he had noticed anything on the office door. The patient remembered that he did notice the *mezuzah* and spontaneously interpreted that he was concerned that Jacobs could be a phony Jew like Mr. K. This was followed by an awareness that possibly it was the former tenant, not Jacobs, who put the *mezuzah* there. At this point Jacobs, putting all of Mr. V.'s associations together, realized that Mr. V. was trying to deny his Jewishness, an issue that had not been explored. Perhaps, Jacobs thought, he and Mr. V. shared the same problem about Jewishness.

While palpating his abdomen, the patient once again returned to Mr. K. and his observation that Mr. K.'s wife was an insensitive, irritable mother. Jacobs recalled at this moment that Mr. V. at 2½ or 3 years of age had had an umbilical hernia that had been treated nightly by binding the abdomen with painfully tight gauze bandages. Jacobs also had a memory of himself being hit in the face by a baseball at the age of 8, mirroring the patient's childhood trauma.

Jacobs pointed out that Mr. V.'s nonverbal gesture and Mr. V.'s observation of Mrs. K.'s irritated diapering of her infant while at the K.s' home were all connected to the patient's traumatic hernia experience. The patient then inveighed against the K.s' having had a bris, the ritualized Jewish circumcision of an infant son. He felt that this was a terribly barbaric, useless surgery. He wondered how Jacobs felt about this ritual.

Before Jacobs could offer an interpretation involving all the preceding elements, Mr. V. offered his own clever synthesis. He stated that Jacobs was going to tell him that he, Mr. V., was angry at Jacobs for moving to a fancy East Side office, and was afraid of Jacobs's retaliating for the expressed anger and that Jacobs, as a possible Orthodox Jew, might perform a circumcision on him and produce a hernia as well.

Jacobs inwardly admired the patient's adroit, intuitive grasp of the dynamics, yet he felt let down. He recalled the legendary football coach Vince Lombardi, who said, "The best defense is a good offense." This image led Jacobs to make the interpretation that Mr. V. had to beat Jacobs to the punch, to control the situation as a defense against castration anxiety.

Mr. V. responded to Jacobs's interpretation with an association expressing his admiration for the Israeli air force's great military competence. The session ended with Mr. V. offering congratulations on the new office and praise for the decor.

According to the Kleinian model, our inner phantasy world is created through introjection and projection. Mr. V. has no doubt introjected his indifferent, self-centered parents and his rejecting, humiliating older brother. He projects them into the external world. Jacobs, of course, has his own inner phantasy world in the service of understanding and apt interpretive work.

Most likely, the patient, having introjected his parents and older brother, feels indifferent to his own success and has a strong, self-centered drive to be indifferent to and disdainful of the success of others. Mr. V. has not been adequately nourished emotionally during the paranoid-schizoid position; consequently he feels empty and greedy. His greediness, I suspect, is what compels him to charge furiously into Jacobs's office. He desperately and angrily wants to scoop out of Jacobs the idealized breast, the nurturance or good he did not receive as an infant. His projective identifications into Jacobs are very strong and cause Jacobs to feel insecure about his office, his clothes, and his Jewishness. Mr. V. is filled with envy and he tries to defend against his envy by devaluating his older brother, Mr. K., and Jacobs's new office. Mr. V. feels persecuted by his parents, who damaged him through the circumcision rites and his oppressive abdominal hernia treatment. His infantile experiences seem to have had more bad in them than good, that is, indifferent, self-involved parents, hernia, and an older brother who mistreated him. Just as the patient feels phony and bad inside, he projects this conviction into his older brother, Jacobs, and Mr. K. The patient's resentment toward Orthodox Jewry or Jewishness may be his attempt to expel his bad parents and brother; to be like an English gentleman seemingly accomplishes this goal. To prevent Jacobs from persecuting him as the bad breast/mommy, he works mightily to control Jacobs through criticism, disdain, and rivalry, for example, through his integrative interpretation before Jacobs can interpret.

Mr. V.'s ego uses splitting very intensively along the following lines:

1. The self that is inadequate and worried about being an impostor versus the critical, arrogant, contemptuous, envious, controlling self.
2. The angry, persecuting self versus the needy, greedy, empty, damaged self.
3. The concerned and repairing self versus the indifferent, self-centered self.

The patient manifests aspects of the depressive position at the end of the session when he praises and congratulates Jacobs on the decor of the new office. He indirectly acknowledges the good in Jacobs as a Jew and an analyst when he compliments the Israeli air force. He also shows concern for Mrs. K.'s mistreated infant, for example, his observation of her irritable, impatient attitude toward her child.

The transferences are as follows:

1. An arrogant, controlling, rivalrous, critical, envious defense against an idealized breast/mommy.
2. A perception of the breast/mommy analyst who withholds needed nourishment.
3. A greedy admiration for the capable, strong, accomplishing breast/mommy analyst.

Jacobs's countertransferences are, in the main, reactions to the chronic, massive, projective identifications put into him by Mr. V. These are as follows:

1. Insecurity about his Jewishness and his appearance and envy of the patient's appearance.
2. Intimidation and anxiety about being greedily invaded and controlled.
3. Competitive rivalry and anger with the patient as Jacobs's rageful, threatening father.
4. An identification with the patient's emotionally and physically damaged infantile self.
5. Admiration for the patient's intuitive self that so quickly assimilated and integrated correctly the diverse dynamics in the session.

Although Jacobs does not refer to the Kleinian model and, in fact, rigorously restricts himself almost exclusively to describing the session's clinical interplay between him and the patient, his interpretations reflect the Kleinian emphasis on the undoing of splitting. For instance, Jacobs points out Mr. V.'s own wish to move to a nicer locale, contradicting his contempt for both Jacobs's and Mr. K.'s move. Above all else, Jacobs's fine clinical vignette reflects and demonstrates the significance of the Kleinian concepts of envy, projective identification, splitting and reparation — central ideas applied in their work daily by Kleinian therapists.

Jacobs, unlike Mr. V., waits patiently for his unconscious to bring him "gifts" of insight and understanding. His awareness of his phantasy world more within the depressive position is not hampered by a feverish, disruptive envy or mounting sense of inner frustrating persecutions. Therefore, Jacobs can be totally aware of and use derivatives of his phantasy world more patiently, completely, and competently than Mr. V.

If we consider the image of the sea in the following lines by Anne Morrow Lindbergh (1955) as symbolic of the unconscious within the therapist and the patient, the writer beautifully captures Jacobs's optimal analytic stance — one, of course, embraced by many contemporary Kleinian therapists.

> The sea does not reward those who are too anxious, too greedy, or too impatient. To dig for treasures shows not only impatience and greed, but lack of faith. Patience, patience, patience, is what the sea teaches. Patience and faith. One should lie empty, open, choiceless as a beach waiting for a gift from the sea. [p. 17]

2

Projective Identification

WHAT IS PROJECTIVE IDENTIFICATION?

Kleinian therapy relies quite heavily on the concept of projective identification (Klein 1946). It refers to a splitting process during which the good and bad parts of the self are expelled from the ego in the form of love or hate into external objects.

The individual who uses projective identification experiences a fusion with the external object.

If the bad part of the self is projected along with hate

then the patient feels paranoid anxiety and persecuted by the external object. The patient will also feel that the external object will attempt to force the bad parts back into him.

The therapist has to distinguish between projective identification as a form of communication and projective identification as a means of expulsion of unwanted parts of the self into the external object; this becomes a means of taking over the object and controlling it.

WHAT IS AN EXAMPLE OF THE POWER OF PROJECTIVE IDENTIFICATION?

As Dr. Nagy came into the room for therapy, I noticed that she seemed dazed. She confirmed my hunch by announcing that she was feeling "spacy."

The patient, a 40-year-old psychologist, had just come from work. I asked her to elaborate on her "spacy" feeling.

"I'm not sure why I feel this way" was her first remark.

I urged, "Well, tell me what's happened today."

"I spoke to my sister this morning. She was very aggravated with my mother. When my sister is angry with my mother she will say, 'I'm angry with your mother.' "

"Your?"

"Yes, 'your.' That's her way of dissociating herself from our mother. It seems my mother fell in the tub and possibly cracked a rib. She called my sister complaining of pain. So naturally my sister wanted to help her. Of course, my mother made things difficult."

"In what way?"

"She said she didn't want to do anything even as she

complained of the pain. My sister called the doctor, who prescribed a chest brace. But that didn't end the problem. My mother insisted on going to a particular pharmacy not close by, because there is a woman there who treats her like she's special. My sister drove there and then my mother got into a fight with the woman over the price and walked out in a huff without the brace."

I waited.

"Oh, yes," the patient continued, "I just remembered. There's this mother who has a 13-year-old, very disturbed adolescent, and the school wanted to throw her out because she's so difficult to handle. I had interviewed this mother and during the course of the interview she mentioned that she had been born on a boat containing Jewish refugees fleeing the Nazis. This same boat was featured in a movie. It grabbed the world's attention when the British refused to allow it to disembark in Palestine. The refugees would have been forced to return to Europe where they would, of course, be murdered by the waiting Germans. I just melted. I wanted to help her. I checked around, found this top-notch special school for her daughter that was willing to take her. It took me about two hours to get this done. She went with her daughter to the school and just before I came here she called me. She vilified the special school and said, 'No one wants to help me.' She accused me of saying that she was an unfit mother and of trying to hurt her daughter. Then she said that she was going to send her daughter to Mexico to a sister-in-law, and her husband was angry with her. She ended by saying that she needed a psychiatrist."

Dr. Nagy paused. "I thought, 'That's good. That's the first positive thing the parent has said.' Okay, so I go ahead and line up a psychiatrist, then just before I come here I call her to give her the name of the doctor and she says she doesn't need a psychiatrist now; she is going to a lady she heard at a lecture who says she can reduce stress. Again she said, 'There's nobody out there who is helping me.' When I hung up the phone, I took a walk to try to clear my head, but when I returned to my office I just couldn't concentrate."

I thought as I listened to the patient that my head was becoming clogged and I could very well understand how she had become "spacy." I remembered that when I was a child, my mother, who had come as an adult to this country and apparently had never learned to read, had complained frequently about her illiteracy. She would repeatedly say, "If only I could read, there isn't anything I couldn't accomplish!" One summer, at age 8, I decided finally to teach my mother to read. I patiently began to show her the basics and quickly realized that she really did not want to learn. My head had become clogged with puzzlement, anger, and frustration at my mother's double message, my reaction to a typical communication of the "help-rejecting complainer." I now recognize that whenever my head is clogged, I am responding to a patient's projective identification, a cry for help put into me followed by a massive, defensive effort to thwart my aid.

In a short period of time Dr. Nagy experienced massive persecutions from two people, her mother and the parent. Functioning solely within the paranoid-schizoid position, they put into the patient, through projective identification, huge amounts of anger and guilt-producing statements. They also put ego-dismembering, sadistic impulses into her. The patient's "spacy" feeling was the consequence of being the container for both her frustrating mother and the parent she had so vainly tried to assist or rescue. Increasing the patient's confusion, these two (Dr. Nagy's mother and the parent) disrupted the connecting links between the thoughts of the patient in her attempt to be a soothing container to them.

I said to Dr. Nagy, "The patient was like your mother, who constantly asks you to help her and then gives you a hard time. You have told me so many times how exasperated you felt and how it takes you a long time to gather your thoughts so as to function minimally after an encounter with her."

What I failed to see sufficiently was that the patient's anxiety was part of the negative transference. She was worried that I would be unable to reliably and safely contain her anxiety, which might destroy me.

I think I failed to see the negative transference because I was not free of my childhood frustration with my mother's blocking my helpful efforts and was possibly made anxious that I would not function well here as an adequate container for the patient.

WHAT IS AN EXAMPLE OF PROJECTIVE IDENTIFICATION USED IN AN EVACUATIVE MANNER?

Each session Mrs. Edelman (the patient discussed on page 151 and in Chapter 12) began by listing all the emotional atrocities perpetrated upon her by her husband during their thirty-five years of marriage. He criticized her appearance, her housework, her job. If she brought home news of a promotion or a note of appreciation from her boss, he would say, "So what! You're in a job where they were so desperate they would take anybody." Supposedly, Mrs. Edelman's husband was so physically handicapped that he was never able to work full-time. While Mrs. Edelman worked full-time and had to shop for food as well, her husband devoted his day to weight lifting, television, and talk-radio shows. I was able, after a year of once-per-week therapy, to accurately anticipate the marital interaction of Mrs. Edelman and her husband. The husband would inevitably criticize and the patient would retaliate, and then they would be off and running. Mrs. Edelman's tolerance for emotional abuse was truly astounding.

During the sessions I would attempt to interpret her need to be attached to pain and help her become aware of her capacity to be on her own should she choose. I also tried to interpret the basis for her perpetual surprise when her husband predictably disparaged her and displayed massive narcissism and cruelty. I quickly noticed that the patient really did not want to listen to me. Filled with so much pain, self-pity, frustration, and rage, she merely wanted to expel her despair and outrage into me. I realized that there would be many sessions ahead before Mrs. Edelman could introject, let alone integrate, any insight. In the meantime, taking in the patient's internal world and distressing affects, I had to wait and contain her evacuative projections until the time arrived when a healthy part of her self could reach for insight.

The patient reminded me of my mother, who would tearfully tell me how much she had suffered before she married my father and how much she had suffered now because of my father's family. I was influenced by my mother to say something to her that would solve her problem, some glorious insight. I intuitively knew and ultimately came to realize that by just listening and not trying to resolve her problems I was helping her. My awareness at the time of the valuable role of listening to depression and anxiety and remaining calm inwardly, of course, did not yet reflect any knowledge of Bion's valuable contribution of the container/contained concept.

CAN YOU ILLUSTRATE PROJECTIVE IDENTIFICATION AS A RESISTANCE?

Things were not going well for Mrs. Vail, a 39-year-old masochistic woman, in once-per-week therapy. Her marriage and business were both failing and she had to supplement the family's meager income by waitressing. At her part-time job, the patient met Mr. X., also unhappily married. She accepted his invitation to have lunch and they discovered they shared similar unhappy marriages.

Mrs. Vail, married to a much older man, did wonder momentarily in therapy why she was now going in the opposite direction in terms of age disparity. Why was she now attracted to a married man eighteen years younger than she? Mr. X. had a young daughter as did the patient, and they both related that their children were keeping them in their marriages. Mr. X.'s wife was also openly having an affair and Mr. X. strongly wanted to end his marriage.

During the session in which all the above was disclosed, Mrs. Vail kept avoiding the consequences of Mr. X.'s mysterious recent remark that there was something he wished to tell her that was vital, but it would have to wait for a more propitious moment. He would say something like, "When I tell you this, I'm not sure you will be able to handle it," or "I don't think you will want to be with me when I tell you more about myself."

The therapist could not reach enough of the patient's observing ego to have her understand how she apparently was not allowing in self-concern and the therapist as the healthy, critical, and internal part of her self. Mrs. Vail was enacting elements of the paranoid-schizoid position: the preservation

of an idealized object, Mr. X., and the destructive attack on
the therapist, who was the split-off part of the patient's self-
preservative, properly responsive, concerned, adaptive self.

HOW DOES COUNTERTRANSFERENCE RELATE TO A THERAPIST'S PROJECTIVE IDENTIFICATION INTO A PATIENT?

Mrs. Rad, a 30-year-old teacher, was a very light-skinned
African American who entered therapy because of depression and marital difficulties. She described her major conflict
as shame versus affection. What she meant by this was that
she was being torn between being ashamed of having married
a very black man and the recognition that he was a caring,
loving husband.

As therapy unfolded, the patient revealed a lifelong
phantasy of being white, with all the "superiority" it conno-
tated. She imagined that if she had married a white man she
could have passed for white and her life would have been so
much better. She had a repetitive dream since marriage of
soaking in a tub and feeling nice and clean when someone
poured a stream of feces into the water. She always awakened tense and frightened. Mrs. Rad saw her husband as
more primitive because of his darker skin color. She recognized in therapy that she would provoke him, that is, put into
him the projective identification of anger, and, when he
lashed out, she would accuse him of being a "Neanderthal."

The patient brought in a gift, a painted sculpture, which
had been given to her by her husband, and which depicted a

woman with a half-black and half-white face. I asked her for associations to the present. Mrs. Rad related sadly to a woman who used black-and-white reasoning and with her preoccupation with being white or black.

Based on Mrs. Rad's depressive affect, reduced evacuative projections, and greater capacity for concern—all concomitants of the depressive position—I decided to bring to her attention all the elements relating to her central conflict of race identity and ambivalence toward her husband. I made this decision since we had been working on this issue for a long time and I judged that the patient's ego was in a state of receptive reflectiveness. I tried to put it all together interpretively: her sense of feeling soiled by her "primitive" husband, her devaluation of him, and her idealization of herself as the pure princess deserving a white prince. Her associations to my attempt at integrating her splitting appeared confirmatory and I felt inwardly triumphant and exhilarated at having so nicely delivered a potent insight that was so well received.

The session was drawing to a close and Mrs. Rad, standing at the door, turned and languidly said, "So what does it all mean?" This startling question was like a pin deflating me in my prideful elation like a balloon. It also made me recognize that I had countertransferred by colluding with a split-off part of the patient that represented Mrs. Rad's misunderstanding projected into me. While I was actively working to understand Mrs. Rad, her inactive self was passively remaining inert and sealed off. For the patient, then, my partial understanding was good enough, though, of course, it was not really good enough for therapy, since Mrs. Rad, and not I, was supposed to be actively understanding and integrating the split-off parts of her self.

Also mentioned under the topic of resistance is the observation of Betty Joseph (1989). She noted that there are patients who split off their healthy, positive selves as in Mrs.

Rad's case; the desire is manifested to retain their lifeless, destructive selves committed to devaluating therapy. The patient could avoid envy of my potency as she did with her husband's potency by allowing others to labor at understanding while she remained the detached, amused onlooker. Her final remark brought to the surface my countertransference, a magical wish to repair her as well as my excessive need to accept total responsibility for change. I had projected into Mrs. Rad my strong desire to integrate insights, undo split-off aspects of the self, and wish to change. However, good therapy requires a collaboration, not a magical performance by therapist and patient.

As I was working with Mrs. Rad, Jews and blacks were generally drawing further apart. Skirmishes and tension between the two groups were headlined each day in all the media. I may have wished unconsciously to prove to the patient that I, a Jew, could be good, the idealized one. To magically restore the previously good relationship between the Jew and the black may have been in back of my countertransference with the accompanying inappropriate self-congratulation and excessive therapeutic zeal.

GIVE AN EXAMPLE OF HOW A PATIENT'S EXTERNAL OBJECTS MAY USE PROJECTIVE IDENTIFICATION WITH REGARD TO THE PATIENT.

When Ms. Palmer entered the room I could feel the clouds of generated anxiety entering into me.

"I'm so anxious. I don't know who I am," she said. "What right do I have to live in this world?"

I understood the patient's remarks as her typical manner of spoiling any possible good that she might take in. This spoiling left her with a sense of emptiness, depression, and despair. Her self became increasingly fragmented. I decided to focus on her active spoiling maneuvers.

"You make nothing out of everything," I replied. "Who also did this when you were growing up?"

Ms. Palmer was an introspective, hardworking patient and she quickly went back to her childhood.

"Mother made nothing out of me. I was provocative. She was very superstitious. She believed, for instance, that if you walked over a child he would not grow unless you walked back again over him. I would purposely walk over my sister and in spite of mother's insistence not walk back over her again.

"My mother would meet me at the door and say horrendous things to me. I would not know why."

I said that her mother may have confused her because she just wanted to dump her tensions and angers into her. In other words, her mother did not really want to communicate but merely use the patient as a container for her evacuations.

As a child the patient would not accept her role of container to her mother's anxieties and anger but would fight back. With regard to my interpretation she said that her mother had a case of chronic diarrhea. "Perhaps I just didn't want to accept her shit," she said.

Ms. Palmer realized when she was quite young that she could strike back and hurt her mother, and give back the bad dumped into her by her mother with interest. She recognized that she was more powerful and could become very nasty to her mother. When the patient counterattacked, her mother would have a breathing spell and faint.

"So you won a Pyrrhic victory," I observed.

"Yes. My mother would tell my father and he would be angry with me."

I remarked with a wry smile, "So you must have felt like a bad seed."

The patient admitted that she was left feeling guilty, angry, and frustrated. She felt particularly frustrated when she suggested to her mother that she see a doctor for her breathing attacks and her mother repeatedly declined. The patient did not know what to do. Her perception that her mother could obtain help was completely ignored.

I attempted to tie the patient's frustration and initial anxiety over her lack of worth and view of life as meaningless to her parents' treatment of her. Ms. Palmer had introjected her parents and their discounting of her.

The patient added another vital point. Her mother apparently had the magical conviction that she should be understood without words. For instance, she might expect the patient to know how to drive her to a certain part of town by a mere tilting of her head in a general direction. This would inevitably lead to frustration and a quarrel between them.

I said that the patient had introjected her mother's manic defensive functioning and expected to be magically helpful; she could also be controlling or spoiling of any good given to her. Ms. Palmer was persecuting herself for not being able to rescue her mother and for causing her breathing spells and fainting. She attempted to help people who did not want to be helped and who discounted her, that is, her mother, her ex-husband, and her sister. In some instances, her extreme use of denial led to an overly persistent masochistic effort to help when success was just impossible to attain.

HOW ELSE CAN PROJECTIVE IDENTIFICATION SPOIL GIVING AND RECEIVING?

At first the Langs, a young, married couple, appeared reluctant to start the session. They looked at each other, each waiting for the other to begin. Finally Mr. Lang opened up.

"I always feel reluctant to start here as if I have to report on my behavior, but, okay, I'll begin. We had an ugly scene on Saturday. I wanted Jenny to go out, get away from the baby, go with her friend into the city. I left a meeting and just as I got home, I told Jenny to give me five minutes to pick up a tape and get some ice cream and I'll be back so she could go." He paused. "When I came back with time to spare for her to catch a train, she was waiting for me in the street. She tossed the baby at me and called me a lot of names in front of some neighbors. It was really embarrassing. I called her an asshole and she got pissed."

Jenny broke in. "There's another side to this. Do you want to hear my side of the story?"

"Go ahead."

"I had worked hard all morning. I prepared the baby's dinner and left detailed instructions. I wanted to catch the 11:24 A.M. train to New York City. I had to catch that train to meet a friend. Bill knew that. Instead, he comes home five minutes before eleven, doesn't ask if I mind, but goes off and comes back at 11:15."

Bill interrupted and there was some back-and-forth bickering about the time. As they quarreled, I thought that here was another typical *Rashomon* situation where one spouse contradicted the other as to what really had happened. (*Rashomon* is a movie that presents an event seen through the eyes of different protagonists with the result being many different descriptions of the same event.)

Jenny returned to her story. "I had to rush to the train. I almost got killed. I called him from the station to apologize for my angry outburst in front of the neighbors, but Bill didn't take responsibility for making me tense and spoiling my trip into the city."

Bill's ego was split into two parts. One part wanted his wife to have a good time, wanted to give to her. The other part of his self wanted to provoke her, to spoil his giving.

I interpreted the split and Bill appeared to let the interpretation in, but he added that Jenny doesn't really give enough to him.

"I try to give to her. I've gotten better but she doesn't give back to me."

Jenny, of course, took issue with Bill's assertion. "I give to him," she said, "but he spoils the giving," and she offered an example in which she made a sexual overture and Bill reacted with a subtle criticism of her.

Bill seemed to receive thoughtfully my interpretation that he spoiled his giving and receiving. He admitted that his anger at Jenny was responsible for the spoiling.

Although the session had ended with Bill owning his spoiling, which put him into the depressive position, there was still much to explore, clarify, and interpret in subsequent sessions. There was Bill's envy of his wife's capacity to nourish him and his son, his projective identification of his pressures into his wife, his too-quick release of anger, his treatment of his wife as a part-object, and, in general, his narcissistic idealization of himself to the exclusion of his wife's needs.

Jenny's dynamics were more subtle. She did not appear to be operating mainly on a paranoid-schizoid level. However, there did seem to be indicators of manic control and a magical desire for Bill to read her mind and give back to her the exact script she desired.

Their projective identifications into me caused me to feel uncertain as to where each of them stood in relation to the other. Perhaps that was what each of them felt with regard to the other, and my uncertainty might also be a key to why Bill and Jenny had trouble getting started in the session. Bill was not sure how I would feel about him transferentially. Jenny felt more certain about me but was still anxious.

IS THERE ANOTHER EXAMPLE OF HOW PROJECTIVE IDENTIFICATION OCCURS IN MARRIAGE?

The accounting season had ended and Mrs. Tarr expected her husband to return emotionally to her and the children. Instead, it seemed to her that her husband was still frustratingly unavailable.

To begin with, he declined an invitation to go out with another couple to dinner over the weekend. He also told his wife that he might go into the office on Saturday, leaving her in a state of ambiguity as he slept late into Saturday morning. Because she was uncertain as to whether he would work on Saturday she held back on necessary chores and plans as she waited for him to awaken.

By the time they came to me, the Tarrs were glowering at each other. Mrs. Tarr was angry that her husband had declined the dinner invitation and ruined the weekend with his enigmatic communications. She was also angry that he was angry with her since she felt that she was clearly the victim of her husband's thoughtlessness.

Mr. Tarr was angry with his wife because she was not understanding enough of how drained and depressed he felt at the completion of his intense work schedule. He also felt that he had rejected the dinner invitation for good reasons. He had intended to spend a quiet evening with his family instead of leaving the children again as he had been forced to do because of work.

Each had projected into the other bad (sarcasm, name-calling). Mrs. Tarr had built up resentment during the tax season so that her husband's refusal to go out gave her the opportunity to project into him her resentment; this caused her to experience him as angry with her. She did not give him the opportunity to explain his good intentions. He rid himself of the bad that had accumulated in him by not sharing how depressed and drained he felt. His not sharing was put into his wife in the form of vexing uncertainty. He thereby put the bad, his depression and anger, back into his wife.

Both Mr. and Mrs. Tarr were using the manic defense of magical repair, each wishing that the other would omni-sciently sense and alleviate his or her accumulated distress. Mr. Tarr wanted his wife to know that he was depressed and drained without his telling her, or expecting that she would understand without his fully explaining that he merely wished to renew his emotional ties with the children during a quiet evening at home.

Mrs. Tarr, on the other hand, expected her husband to know without being told that she was buckling under the mounting stress of having to make decisions alone and deal with problems by herself while her husband was immersed in the enveloping burden of work.

They were both functioning within a paranoid-schizoid position where there was little recognition of the separation between objects, coupled with a restricted sensitivity and concern with the totality of the other. My therapeutic task in the session was gradually to clarify the projective identifications, one's manic wish for quick repair by the other, and the unreality of their narcissistic insensitivity to their spouse's individuality and unique tensions.

3

The Container

WHAT IS THE MEANING OF THE CONCEPT *CONTAINER*?

Container or *containment*, a concept originated by Bion (1958, 1959, 1962), refers to the therapist's active set that allows him to integrate the patient's projective identifications. Through containment the therapist, in effect, holds in his mind the patient's material, which is then fed back to the patient via understanding and acceptance, that is, valid interpretations.

Excessive projective identification can lead to a breakdown of the self, causing the patient to misunderstand interpretations. Psychotics, for example, suffer particularly from excessive use of projective identification with a resultant blurring of self and object boundaries.

Powerful projective identifications may even evoke physical sensations in the therapist as well as the conviction that he or she is incompetent and worthless as a professional.

Rosenfeld (1987) makes the important point that projective identification can be defensive not only against envy and aggression but also against a denial of reality. The patient may split off hated, feared parts of his self, evacuate them into the therapist, and then disown possession of them.

WHAT IS AN EXAMPLE?

Mrs. Sager, a narcissistic woman, ran both her business and her marriage aggressively. She was constantly confused as to why her husband, and men in general, would be angry with her since she did not, she felt, do anything to antagonize them.

Toward the end of one session, the patient bolted toward my phone, picked it up and, speaking rapidly, said, "Just one quick phone call, just a minute." I was, needless to say, stunned. As I was recovering, the patient quickly dialed and gave instructions to an employee for the duration of a full minute. As she hung up she complacently commented, "You see it was only just a minute." I could not respond because time had run out in the session and another patient was in the waiting room.

The next session I brought the patient back to the previous one. I asked her how she had felt about using my phone without first asking me for permission. At first she denied that she had done anything improper. I then asked her how she imagined I felt when she took charge of my phone. She hesitated, and with some effort grudgingly speculated that I might have been hurt or angry. I proceeded to show her how this incident reflected her general problem with men in general and her husband in particular. Her brazen, dismissive attitude and her smug rationalization were contributing to her resistance to understanding others' objections to her controlling discounting of their wishes.

The patient's projective identification of her controlling inconsiderateness into me was meant to deny the reality of her aggressive attacks. In addition to Mrs. Sager's detailed descriptions of her vain mother, she also wanted me to know what it felt like when her narcissistic mother had similarly ridden roughshod over her as a child by ignoring her wishes. She had felt persecuted then by her mother and she was now persecuting me and all men. Within the paranoid-schizoid position, Mrs. Sager, seeing me as a part-object, felt she owned my possessions and me. She therefore, expected condoning of her entitlements, not analysis of them. By containing her aggressive projective identification of brazen narcissism into me, I could calmly give back to her, through clarification and interpretation, the destructive consequences of her self-centeredness.

WHAT IS AN EXAMPLE OF A DAMAGED CONTAINER, A THERAPIST'S SEXUAL ACTING OUT?

When a therapist acts out the sexual projective identifications put into him by a patient, any subsequent therapy, and especially the transference, will be tarnished and made inordinately difficult. The unethical therapist has intensified the patient's belief in the controlling power of his or her projective identifications, and has made the exposure of oedipal material extremely difficult in a new therapy. More important, the whole issue of the therapist as a suitable container representing trust, non-exploitation, and safety is impaired and complicated.

The following vignette illustrates the deleterious consequences of an ongoing affair with a former therapist even as the patient, Mrs. Isler, is involved in therapy with a new therapist.

"This patient is in crisis," began Dr. Block. "She has been two years in therapy and during that time she took three months off under mysterious circumstances."

My ears perked up at the mention of the word "mysterious." Dr. Block continued, "She holds a lot of secrets. She is about 50 years old, an average-looking woman. She could do more with herself. She comes across as a nervous, fragile, vulnerable person. There are a number of sides to her, though. She can be demanding, childlike, and impulsive. Another side shows bribery and aggression. Even on the phone she seems to have two different voices. It's scary, like *The Exorcist*. But I don't see her as a multiple personality.

"She wants me to take care of her. She had been in individual therapy and in group for five years. She had an affair with her former therapist, whom she saw nine years ago. The therapist is married and no longer a therapist. I suspect that he was a womanizer, from what the patient has told me about him.

"The patient's marriage has been a disaster. Her husband is teasing and sadistic. He would, for instance, refuse intercourse but would instead masturbate in front of her. She would like to end her marriage but feels unable to support herself financially. Her husband will devaluate her in front of others, causing her great humiliation and embarrassment.

"The patient perceives her former therapist as wonderful in contrast to her husband. She believes her main problem is that he will not marry her. He tells her firmly that their present status of lovers is unchangeable and she must accept these terms if they are to continue their present relationship. He is much older than the patient.

"As a consequence of therapy the patient has become stronger and less desirous of being dependent on or taken care of by a man. However, she is not able to accept her growth and spends many sessions denigrating her lover's wife, whom she perceives as 'plain' and foolishly tolerant of his numerous past affairs. She also becomes angry when she realizes that she is not her former therapist's priority. She oscillates between accepting her status as a lover and not a wife, and wanting in a rage to kill him.

"The present crisis in therapy has occurred because her lover no longer wishes to see her. When the patient strongly approaches him to change his mind, he retreats. She has frequently called him. She doesn't know what to do. She wants him back and wants the present therapist, the supervisee, to help get her lover back. She feels totally alone. She is cut off from her husband and feels terribly dependent on her former rejecting lover again.

"Her family background is as follows: Her mother and the patient are only children, excessively attached to each other. She slept in her mother's bed until she was 6 years old. Her father was not involved and apparently was treated by the patient and her mother as an overgrown child. His nickname in the family was and is 'Daddy boy'."

It is clear that to a great degree the former therapist is behaving like the patient's mother and has breached significant incest-related and ethical boundaries. Just as the patient slept with her mother, she has slept with her former therapist.

However, the former therapist has also behaved like the patient's father — really uninvolved and rejecting.

The patient goes from idealization of the therapist, from "He is wonderful" to "He does not make me enough of a priority." She seems to reach out to men from a paranoid-schizoid position. She selects men who treat women as part-objects. She employs splitting so intensely that the supervisee, her present therapist, almost thinks of her as a multiple personality. She has split her ego along the following lines: a needy, demanding, fragile part versus a bitchy, aggressive part, and a hurting, vulnerable, dependent part versus an active, sadistic part projected into men to whom she becomes significantly attached.

Her envy of her therapist lover's wife eats away at her, and even as she deprecates the wife she diminishes her own growth and strength.

I suggested to the supervisee that he deal with the immediate transference, that is, the patient's wish for the therapist to give her "mysterious" secrets that will magically repair her broken relationship with her lover. I also emphasized that the patient may be trying to control her present therapist and therapy even as she strives to control her former therapist. The patient sees her good being taken away by her former therapist. The patient's spoiling of the good received in her current therapy also needs to be addressed and interpreted.

CAN YOU ILLUSTRATE THE FAILURE AND REPAIR OF THE CONTAINER?

When Mrs. Wade, tormented by chronic fatigue and depression, repeatedly accused me of not connecting with her, I began an intensive self-examination to determine what was going on within myself and the patient to cause this frustrating impasse. I observed initially that the patient was spoiling my interpretations, not willing to take in the good, envious of my potency, and so forth. But soon I began to realize that I did not really want to look more closely at my role to discover a countertransference. Once I shifted attention to my own internal world, I realized that the patient was evoking within me painful memories of my own childhood when I felt emotionally abandoned and perpetually blamed for shortcomings by my own parents. Mrs. Wade had seen my interpretations as blaming and as an abandonment similar to her parents' desertion of her when she was sick with a chronic childhood illness. I recognized that my childhood pain was causing me not to be sufficiently tolerant of the patient's pain. I noticed that whenever Mrs. Wade started to talk about her feelings of abandonment and being blamed, I, falsely assuming the necessity of support and transference interpretations, would come in and cut short her staying with the pain. In other words, I was not permitting the patient the appropriate right to project into me a part of her self that was lonely, abandoned, attacked, and hurting. I was defensively closing off my containing function.

In a subsequent session I told her that I would stay more X ? with her pain and absorb it. I would allow her to go through her anguished memories and not quickly rush in with understanding. The patient visibly relaxed and said, "Now I feel you're connecting with me," and therapy moved past the impasse. The container had finally been restored.

WHAT IS AN EXAMPLE OF A PATIENT RESTORING HER OWN CONTAINING FUNCTIONS?

Mrs. Yanof was a 51-year-old patient who had initially entered therapy because of depression and severe marital difficulties. A few sessions after a dream, she recalled the day residue preceding her dream. When she first told the dream, we had reached a consensus that the dream dealt with painful anticipated loneliness as a consequence of her divorce and ambivalent feelings toward her children.

The patient remembered that during the day preceding the dream, she had had a medical examination. There was a mirror in the room and when she looked at herself, she was shocked by her appearance. The technician kept calling her "dear," the way an old person, she felt, might be treated.

Her associations to the day residue were as follows: She felt old, "over the hill," ready for the scrap heap. She remembered a scene from the movie *Avalon*. At the end of the movie one of the characters, Michael, visits his elderly father, Sam, who is in a nursing home and tells him he is naming his son after him. Sam reminds his son that he is still alive and it is contrary to Jewish tradition to name a child after a living relative. Sam says, "I'm alive."

I asked Mrs. Yanof to give me her understanding of the day residue. She paused thoughtfully. "I guess I'm very concerned with getting older. I look at my mother and she's getting more irrational." She then added that her mother had always seemed irrational to her as a child. She could never reach her. When the patient arrived at early adolescence she developed a passion for Yiddish music. She collected every available record and tape. As she spoke her eyes teared. "The music soothed me. It got me through tough times, the early years of childhood, my terrible marriage. It always amazed me how much the music soothed me. Without it I would have been dead."

In contrast to the patient's initial visible tension and depressing thoughts and feelings about her sense of isolation and loneliness, she appeared relaxed and calm. What had happened?

The patient went back to the nurturing, soothing maternal breast/mommy (Yiddish music), and was contained and calmed. She left the paranoid-schizoid position of perceived external and internal persecution to re-find a significant, past effective means of calming herself, of re-establishing a sense of safety and connectedness. She was able to reduce the split between the external object, her mother, who refused to connect with the patient in a meaningful way, and the mother who perhaps sang Yiddish songs to her in a soothing, empathic manner. Contained empathically by the therapist, she could restore an internal container and not feel spoiled, defective, useless, and discarded. She no longer accepted her painful apprehension that the "living" would treat her as if she were "dead." She was able to remind herself that, just as she was resourcefully able to repair herself successfully in the past, she could continue to do so in the future.

GIVE AN EXAMPLE OF A PATIENT'S PATHOLOGICAL CONTAINER.

Bion's (1959, 1962) concept of container is a very useful explanatory tool, shedding light on some difficult states of anxiety. Here is an example.

Mr. Sacks entered therapy complaining of his debilitating periodic tendency to slide into an anxious state every time he had to talk in a group. "One on one" was fine but a group threw him into an abyss of tension and terror.

As we explored the patient's early childhood and family background, it became more and more apparent that he had had to be a container for huge amounts of anxiety transferred by both his parents. His father, particularly, seemed to be a passive, ineffectual man who could not cope with any stress. He would either run away physically, retreat into a "zombie-like" attitude, or fly into rages. His parents would ask him to decide for them on all family problems. He remembered one instance among many when he was 9 years of age. His parents called upon him to pronounce judgment on whether his ailing grandmother, who lived with them, should be placed in a nursing home. Apparently the patient, pressured to be the family guru, fulfilled his parents' desperate expectation, for he answered "Yes!" very decisively.

I interpreted to Mr. Sacks that he had been thrust into the role of parent to his parents when he was least able to neutralize the massive amounts of rage and tension that they put into him. His parents had idealized him as a prodigy, an omnipotent, omniscient receptacle for all their problems, and the patient had accepted that role. As an adult he was now paying a terrible price, a phobic fear of being in a group. In a group he anticipated being asked to contain its anxieties and issues, and it was just too overwhelming.

Of course I did not interpret all the above at once but did it gradually throughout the course of therapy. We discovered that the patient had also introjected the pathological containing functions of his father. He split his ego in the following way: the precocious, idealized self that could contain anyone's tension versus the feeble, unstable self that could not contain a group's anxieties. Though the patient was mainly at the depressive position in his concern for others and his view of them as total objects, the early-childhood, chronic, massive influx of anxiety placed into him by his parents left him vulnerable to an easy regression to the paranoid-schizoid position. In this position, he experienced persecutory anxiety and the conviction that he was merely a part-object. He was also beset by vexing envious impulses.

level. She is concerned, for instance, that the therapist does not really care about her and she repeatedly devalues therapy. She also accuses the therapist of wasting her time and money, an odd statement since she employs the word "precious" with regard to therapy time.

The patient's ego is split along the following lines: a part of her self that cares versus a part that does not care, a part of the ego that is concerned versus a part that is not, and a part of her ego that is aware of herself and sees the therapist as a total person and a part of her that perceives her self as fragmented and decaying (e.g., sludge, decaying food in childhood home).

Her paranoid anxieties are: terror of nonexistence, abandonment, diffuse identity, conviction of being unloved, and a fear of going crazy. These anxieties are being projected into the therapist, who feels dazed, incompetent, and uncertain about her therapeutic role. The patient also employs manic defenses, attempting to control the therapist as to what should be talked about (e.g., priorities) and impatiently chides the therapist for not magically mind-reading her psyche.

I suggested to the supervisee that she begin drawing attention to the patient's contradictory feelings about therapy. The therapist might ask the patient what she feels about therapy time that is "precious" and therapy time that is a waste of time and money. Is the patient spoiling "precious" therapy time as food was allowed to decay and spoil in her childhood home?

In essence, the Kleinian model heightens the diagnostic process or understanding of the patient by focusing on a central issue, the patient's spoiling of any good that is offered in or out of therapy. The continuation of spoiling only furthers the patient's anxiety of becoming crazy like her parents. Once the supervisee understands how the patient's ego is split she can then move toward helping the patient integrate the split-off parts of her ego.

WHAT IS THE FUNDAMENTAL ANXIETY OF MOST PATIENTS AT THE BEGINNING OF THERAPY?

The main anxiety of the patient is that he or she will drive the therapist crazy or that the therapist will cause craziness in the patient.

Moreover, since the paranoid-schizoid position is characterized by a lack of concern for others, a patient predominantly in this position is not concerned about harming the therapist as much as being injured by the therapist. It is only within the depressive position that the patient is concerned for the therapist's welfare.

IS COUNTERTRANSFERENCE THE KEY TO UNDERSTANDING THE PATIENT?

The key to the proper use of countertransference is the therapist's constant self-awareness of projective identifications put into him by the patient and any excessive unconscious components or defenses apart from either the paranoid-schizoid or the depressive position.

Possible countertransferences are as follows:

1. Originating from the therapist's paranoid-schizoid position, he might countertransferentially put the bad object placed into him by the patient back into the patient.
2. The therapist might experience the patient in black and white terms only.
3. He may experience a lack of concern or responsibility in reaction to the projective identifications put into him.
4. He may perceive the patient as a part-object in response to the part-object projective identifications placed into him by the patient.
5. When the patient places a split-object projective identification into the therapist, the therapist may similarly experience the patient's external objects as split into the all-"bad" or all-"good" objects (e.g., the "bad" mother and/or the "good" father).
6. As the patient places his envy of the therapist into the therapist, the therapist may angrily and unwittingly be blinded by envy of the patient.

In moderation, all the elements of the depressive position are positively correlated with successful treatment. For example, concern for the patient, appropriately felt, is a *sine qua non* of the working alliance. So is the therapist's awareness of the separateness of the patient.

Countertransferences may originate from the depressive position as follows:

1. Excessive concern for the patient.
2. Too much emphasis on the independence of the patient.
3. Too much protectiveness of the patient.
4. Too much guilt — responding to the patient's projective identification of guilt put into the therapist.
5. Too much object constancy (e.g., the therapist obsesses about the patient).
6. Excessive need to repair the patient, that is, rescue.

7. Too many of the therapist's projective identifications put into the patient.
8. Too extensive a sense of responsibility.
9. Too much control over phantasies and impulses. The therapist is uptight and unable to gain enough connection to his inner world so as to understand the patient. He becomes frightened of the patient's regression.
10. The patient's poor reality testing and reasoning placed into the therapist causes him to distort reality and reasoning with regard to the patient.

HOW DOES A KLEINIAN THERAPIST PROCESS THE PATIENT'S MATERIAL?

There are a number of questions posed internally as the Kleinian therapist listens. These are:

1. What is the main position being manifested, paranoid-schizoid or depressive?
2. What are the projective identifications?
3. What kind of splitting is occurring, that is, what kind of ego splitting and external object splitting?
4. How is envy being manifested?
   a. Greed
   b. Spoiling
   c. Despair
   d. Negative Therapeutic Reaction
   e. Cognitive impairment
   f. Devaluation
   g. Rigid idealization
   h. Rivalry

5. What are the transferences? For example, is the therapist seen as impaired or adversely affected by the patient's behavior, unaffected by the patient's material, idealized, rejecting, and so forth.
6. What are the countertransferences?
7. What are the resistances?
8. What is the nature of the bad persecutory parts of the self and the good objects?
9. Can phantasies that defend against other phantasies be delineated?
10. How does the patient use splitting, denial, or idealization?
11. What is the nature of the patient's ego relationships to internal and external objects?
12. What is the nature of the ideal self and the ideal object?
13. What are the aims of projective identification?
    a. To avoid separation
    b. To get rid of the bad self or bad object
    c. To safeguard the good self or good object
    d. To improve the external object
    e. To distort reality (to attack the connection between self and object or the connection between thoughts)
14. What are the anxieties?
    a. Hypochondriacal anxiety caused by reintrojection of persecuting parts of the self and bad objects
    b. Retaliatory attack by attacked object
    c. Anxiety of depletion of goodness through projection of good parts
    d. Anxiety of having parts of oneself imprisoned and controlled by objects
    e. Acute anxiety (disintegration as the ego's attempts to ward off anxiety)
15. How effective is the therapist as a "container"?

16. What position, Paranoid-Schizoid or Depressive, is being monitored?
   A. Characteristics of Paranoid-Schizoid Position (PS)
      (1) Persecution by internal object or part of self
      (2) Excessive splitting
      (3) Excessive projective identification
      (4) "Black and white" reasoning (no ambivalence toward external object)
      (5) Lack of acceptance of responsibility
      (6) Lack of concern for others
      (7) Increased envy
      (8) Relating to self or external object as part object
   B. Characteristics of Depressive Position (D)
      (1) Concern for external object and self
      (2) Awareness of independence of object
      (3) Protection of object from destructiveness
      (4) Object constancy
      (5) There can be mourning or pining
      (6) Guilt
      (7) A need to repair an impaired or damaged relationship
      (8) Projective identifications are lessened
      (9) Greater self-awareness regarding impulses and phantasies
      (10) Greater distinction between reality and phantasy
      (11) Diminished omnipotent feelings
      (12) Increased sense of responsibility
      (13) Increased control of impulses
      (14) Greater respect for individuality
      (15) Conscience becomes less severe and persecutory, more helpfully forgiving
      (16) Defense mechanisms are more neurotic (i.e., inhibition, repression, and displacement)
      (17) Capacity to reason on an abstract level increases.

(18) Capacity to repair relationships increases
(19) Belief in capacity to love and in potential improves
(20) Excessive denial (manic defense) against internal world
(21) Excessive manic defense against any dependency; may have devaluation and splitting
(22) Excessive manic defense against guilt or ambivalence
(23) Manic attempts to control and triumph over object; possible contempt, ridicule
(24) Manic reparation characterized by magical, quick repair of self or object

HOW DOES A KLEINIAN THERAPIST PROCESS THE PATIENT'S MATERIAL?

For therapists of diverse schools, the best understanding may occur away from the treatment room. I have found, for example, that I obtain insights into the dynamics of a session when I am involved in a routine, repetitive task such as shaving. Such was the case with Mr. Parker.

During the session Mr. Parker reported a dream in which an Asian man shorter than he was having sex with his girlfriend. This man had an unusually large penis. The patient's girlfriend was having an orgasm. He awakened so angry that he almost felt compelled to call his girlfriend and ragingly accuse her of betraying him.

Mr. Parker felt very insecure about the size of his penis and attributed his girlfriend's inability to achieve orgasm as the fault of his inadequate penis. He wondered if the dream represented a mere wish to sexually satisfy his girlfriend.

However, "Why," he thought, "an Asian man smaller than me?" He recognized the possibility that his anger at his girlfriend's betrayal of him in his dream might have represented his wish to sexually "cheat" so as to give another woman an orgasm.

During the same session, Mr. Parker commented with some embarrassed hesitation that he wanted to tell me that there was a trait of mine that bothered him. An instance of this was my recent disclosure that my son, a psychologist, had encountered a similar professional problem as the patient and had dealt successfully with it. The patient felt that my personal revelation, which I meant to reassure him, instead had distracted and angered him. He wished that I would no longer reveal anything about my personal life. I felt guilty and stupid. I reassured him that I heard his grievance and that it was valid. I had negatively countertransferred.

A few days later while I was shaving, the thought struck me that the Asian man in Mr. Parker's dream was both me and my son. I realized that the Buddha statue in my office and other Asian artifacts were incorporated in the person of the Asian man who gave an orgasm to the patient's girlfriend. Mr. Parker was enviously seeing me and my son as more potent than himself. We could both receive and give "good," unlike him. When he criticized my personal disclosure, his annoyance, valid in part, also incorporated a need to destroy my potency in order to mitigate his envy. I had missed this dynamic.

In the session that followed, the patient, in response to my interpretation of his envy of my potency, admitted that he did indeed envy a colleague who looked like me. This man was about to secure an advanced degree that the patient craved. The degree, in his mind, conferred prestige, money, and power. The patient felt that he knew as much if not more than the colleague. Yes, he envied me and his criticism of me was meant to "cut" me down to size. He felt guilty about that. He then went on to describe how he had felt panicky at a recent meeting where he was the only male. His boss and her superior were there. They were, he believed, castrating females. He wondered if his panic was related to the sense that they were potent and to his envy of them.

He then went back to his insecurity about the small size of his penis. Toward the second half of the meeting, the patient somehow felt no panic. I interpreted at this point, "You were active then, made suggestions, and the women took them in."

"Yes," he added, "they liked my ideas, which came from knowledge of other areas they did not know."

"So," I added, "You did not envy them any more."

"Right! I was potent."

I continued, "In your dream the Asian man representing me and my son knew how to satisfy your girlfriend. You may envy my knowing or understanding of you."

"That's why I want a Ph.D." he replied. Like the classical model and other psychoanalytic theories, Kleinian therapy, beginning in the initial session, considers the therapist's valid interpretations to be the main therapeutic vehicle for change. They communicate understanding, acceptance, and concern. The therapist becomes a non-anxious container of the patient's mind, interpreting the anxieties and internal object relations, and reducing projective identifications, splitting, defenses, idealization, greed, and envy. The main interpretive emphasis, however, is always on the immediate transference.

Here are some more examples of how a Kleinian therapist listens and processes the patient's material during an initial session.

Mr. Quinn, 34 years old, was quite overweight, and his first explanation for why he had initiated therapy centered on his obesity. "I think I shove food into me to push down my anger."

"What do you mean?"

"If I didn't eat I would kill somebody. I have genuine sympathy for Joel Rifkin [a mass murderer of women]." He continued, "I have two choices. I could kill others or kill myself by increasing my already existing diabetes—and I don't think I would like to die that kind of death."

"Tell me about your rage."

"I feel like I could kill—particularly women."

"What about your anger toward women?"

"I'll explain this way. I went to a nude bar and if you pay money, you get to dance with a girl and even get to go to a private place where the girl will dance just for you. I just talked to her. She told me about herself and I did the same. I felt more connected to her than I did to my own wife.

"Being with my wife is like being alone. She may have feelings but I don't feel her feelings. There's no sex and no feelings.

"I could lose weight and control my diabetes, but I don't think anything would change in my marriage."

"How so?"

"She avoids me. Yesterday, for instance, she said that she was tired during the day so we didn't talk or do much. Then when I start readying myself to go to sleep, she wakes up. She doesn't sleep with me. She has excuses. Last night she said that she couldn't sleep with me because she had gas."

I intervened at this point, "I don't know anything about your parents." This was an invitation to the patient to describe his family of origin.

"I was the invisible man. My brother, three years older, was like my father, a barroom brawler, always fighting in school, good mechanically like my father, and into drugs.

"My father looked at my brother proudly as a 'chip off the old block.'

"Both my mother and father ignored me. When I was 12, I found this other family down the block and spent all my time with them. They were a large, loving family. I could talk to them and they treated me like a son. I'm still close to them. My parents never even questioned me as to why I spent so much time away from home!

"I say I'm the invisible son and here's another example. For my father's last birthday I got him a nice present and a card. I put both in front of his plate. When he came down for breakfast, he sat there and did not open his gift or card until after eating. When he opened the gift and card signed by me and my wife, he looked at my wife and said, 'Thank you for the gift.' I was right next to her. He didn't say anything to me!"

I could feel the patient's pain, sadness, rejection, and outrage as he described his father's bizarre selective inattention to him.

The patient's wife, B., is inordinately immersed in her career, which she passionately enjoys. There are no children, nor is there any desire for a child on the part of either one of them.

I asked, "So what do you want to get out of therapy?"

"I want a better life. I want a better marriage. I want to feel better about myself. I think if I feel better about myself, I'll believe I deserve better than what I have.

"If I lose the weight, I'll feel better and expect more from my wife. If she doesn't give emotionally to me, then I will have to consider ending the marriage. I envy other couples who seem happy.

"I don't want to break up the marriage, but I don't want to be the invisible man again, which I feel I am in relation to my wife."

At the end of the session, I said, "Let's you and I work together to help you become more visible to yourself and others."

If we look at the patient's material from a Kleinian vantage point, what seems most striking is the absence of the good, nourishing breast. Both parents emotionally absented themselves from the patient and obviously discounted him. I would expect that all the concomitants of the paranoid-schizoid position would be intensified and exist within him, for example, part-object perception of himself, envy, and so on.

Mr. Quinn feels empty and uses food as a substitute for the idealized breast/mommy, but this introjection is toxic, a poisoned breast. He is obese, unappealing physically to his wife and to himself. In addition, he has a life-threatening illness, diabetes, which if uncontrolled will result in his being truly invisible, that is, dead.

He treats himself like a part-object by frequenting porn shops and nude bars. He hopes that heightened sexual feelings will somehow substitute for the absent soothing good breast and increase his ego strength. In this way he desires to avoid fragmentation and annihilation of his self. He once faced this same annihilation in his family, but healthily reached out for another, more giving breast, a substitute family.

It is still too early to tell if he has projected into his wife a split-off part of himself, the "dead" son-child, with the result that she would be "dead" to him. Or that he is behaving like his parents and rejecting her as they rejected him.

He can move into the depressive position as demonstrated by his own report that what he enjoyed most was talking, that is, connecting emotionally to the woman in the nude bar. He wants a more total relationship, not one where he is either made "dead" or treated contemptuously as a part-object. Threatened by possible fragmentation by his wife and family's treatment of him, he struggles to keep down the rageful drive to fragment others.

I realized that the patient wished to introject me as the ego-enhancing breast so that he could finally decide what to do about his marriage. He did project the hurting, rejected part of his self into me and I, as the container, attempted to give back to him, with my final remark from the depressive position, a hope that he would relate more to himself as a total person, have more appropriate concern for himself, and expect more consideration from others. He would, therefore, no longer have to envy other couples' happiness. Lessened envy, in turn, would diminish his hopelessness and conversely increase hope.

During the initial interview I also registered his splitting. Mr. Quinn has a self that wants to control his life, his weight, his diabetes, and his marriage, versus a self that wants to destroy itself, to disintegrate him as his family managed to do to him from infancy through adulthood. He has a self that wants to "kill" others, particularly women, versus a self that would rescue itself, creating a better relationship with his wife. He also has a self that maintains treatment of itself as a discounted part-object, versus a self that wants a more total, considerate relationship. All these splits would have to be attended to, interpreted, and worked through, fostering an increased integrative status concomitant with the depressive position.

There is also an oedipal aspect. The patient was treated as the excluded one as a child. His family closed ranks and made him "invisible." His wife appears to have closed ranks with her career and similarly made him "invisible." Mr. Quinn colludes with his wife's rendering of him as nonexistent by his "shoving food into his mouth," thus moving inexorably toward a possible diabetic coma.

I anticipated the following transferences: One is seeing me as a part-object, invisible, out of control, envious, and rageful; these are all the products of the projective identifications of his disowned self into me. Another transference is his perceiving me to be treating him as invisible and as a part-object.

I would need to be aware of the following countertransference: an excessive introjection of the hurt, discounted part of the patient projected into me, which would cause me to become very angry at significant external objects, for example, his wife and his parents. If I allowed this countertransference to govern my role as his therapist, I would miss what Mr. Quinn does to maintain himself pathologically in the paranoid-schizoid position.

I think that the prognosis is good, since the patient shows concern with himself, wants a total relationship, and is anxious about hurting others. He did at one time make a heroic attempt to escape the blatant pathology of his family by entering into another, more healthy, family. He can introject the good breast/mommy, wants to work on himself, and does evidence reparative tendencies; these are all healthy elements of the depressive position.

Here is another example of an initial session and a diagnostic application of the Kleinian model to the patient's material.

The patient, Mrs. Haas, a divorced teacher, 42 years old, entered therapy because of anxiety attacks and overwhelming hypochondriacal fears. She has two daughters, 12 and 14, and has been divorced for seven years. She is in a graduate program in human relations.

Mrs. Haas described her ex-husband as a "total washout." From the beginning of the marriage she had to assume the entire responsibility of managing the family's financial resources and had to be the sole parent to the children emotionally.

According to the patient, she became morbidly hypochondriacal a few years ago. She believes she behaves this way because she feels totally responsible for everything that happens around her.

Mrs. Haas is an only child. She felt closer to her father than to her mother. Her father died two years ago. She considers her mother a "total emotional wreck." Her mother is depressed and "strange."

She has one close, best friend, Mrs. W. "I drive her crazy. She is happily married. She is a strong person." They have been friends for fourteen years.

I asked the patient to describe her panic attacks in more detail.

"When I have an anxiety attack I have a lump in my throat," she said. I feel shaky and my heart starts to beat fast."

Mrs. Haas admits that she becomes nervous over money but does not panic. She will panic regarding any health problem that she suspects she may have or that her daughters may have.

Asked to give more details about her parents, the patient said, "My father was always in control, while my mother was always out of control. My mother relied on my father. My father never panicked. I learned not to share anything with my mother. I can easily recall frequent expressions of anxiety on my mother's face whenever I talked to her about any problem no matter how minor.

"My father was the complete and total boss. My mother worshiped him. She had trouble handling things. My mother felt that my father was brighter than she was.

"Any siblings?" I asked.

"No. I was an only child, but I never realized that I was an only child. I had friends. I was not home much.

"When my mother was pregnant with me it was a bad pregnancy. She was ill but she's *always* complained. Whenever I'm with her we fight like crazy. She's a terrible 'downer.'

She's good with my kids, though. She's protective of them. She's also rigid."

"Tell me about your husband."

"I met my husband in college. We got married in my junior year. He said that he had graduated but he really never finished. He really had only taken two courses. Lucky for him, his father had a lucrative business. His father died a couple of months ago.

"My ex-husband lives with his mother. Emotionally he's about 18 or 19. He's never progressed beyond that age. He hasn't worked for many years. His mother sends for the children. I try very hard not to put him down."

Asked about work, Mrs. Haas said, "I love my job. I like teaching. I love kids and my own children are a source of joy to me, but I worry about them, especially my older daughter. She shares everything with me."

"Were you ever in therapy before?"

"Last fall I saw a social worker, two or three times a week. It didn't work out."

"How come?"

"I don't know. Maybe I just don't have enough faith that therapy works."

What can we discern from a Kleinian perspective about this patient?

There seems to be a continuing surfacing and resurfacing of two internal objects, mother and father, in Mrs. Haas's material and her life.

One parent, her father, is the good, idealized object. He is portrayed as controlled, strong, calm, intelligent, and capable.

Her mother, on the other hand, is described as a bad object. She was always out of control, easily panicked and idealizing of the patient's father.

Having these two significant objects in her internal

world, Mrs. Haas probably will evidence the following splits: a controlled, strong, capable, independent self versus a panicky, dependent self. In this connection, her hypochondriacal anxieties may be the outcome of attacks of her introjected bad breast/mommy, who offers little soothing and ego strength. The patient's mother does not sound like a good reliable container. The patient admits she could not share anything with her mother. Perhaps this explains why the patient has such a strong sharing relationship with her older daughter. It sounds reparative and appears to be an ✓ opportunity to be a good father and mother to her daughter as well as to herself.

I suspect that having a mother who was a poor container has intensified some elements in the paranoid-schizoid position. The idealization of the father by both the patient and her mother may conceal some marital discord. This will have to be probed. The patient appears to have selected a husband more like her mother than like her father. What needs to be ✓ examined further is the possibility that her father may have some of the same pathology as her ex-husband.

Her ex-husband, the patient claims, fooled her. Her father may have fooled her as well. There is no mention of envy of the father, but the patient may have dealt with her envy by transferentially selecting a husband-father whom she could reject contemptuously as an irresponsible, mother-dependent, immature "child."

I suppose the patient may see me at times as her idealized father and project into me strength, dependability, and competence. Later as she projects her mother introject into me, she may experience me as weak, panicky, out of control, and incompetent.

Mrs. Haas's previous therapy may have foundered upon her projections of the maternal introject into the last therapist. As the patient puts it, "I lost faith that therapy works."

I will have to watch out that I do not collude with the

patient's projective identifications into me and either become controlling like her idealized father or panicky, with a disintegrating ego, like her mother.

The prognosis is good. The patient seems mainly in the depressive position. She shows concern for her daughters and is capable of accepting responsibility — too much so at times. She demonstrates reparative tendencies, for example, her relationship with her daughters and good use of a friend, Mrs. W, a good container. She may, however, be warning me that she will fill me with overwhelming tensions (depressive position), and hopes that I will be strong enough, like her friend, not to be driven crazy (a typical depressive-position anxiety) at the beginning of therapy.

Here is another initial interview:

Ms. Macy's reason for entering therapy was depression. She felt that she was going through the motions of living during the day. She looked at everything as a chore. She had divorced a year and a half ago and had a 2½-year-old daughter.

The patient had gotten engaged right after college. The engagement was short, accompanied by many mixed feelings toward her fiancé. Her future husband seemed very sweet at first, especially in comparison to a former boyfriend who had been verbally abusive to her. Ms. Macy's fiancé gave her freedom, and they seemed to be great friends. However, their sexual relationship began to deteriorate soon after they were married. Her husband just seemed to want oral sex and nothing else. The patient took charge of her husband's business, experiencing him as inadequate and childlike in his management of life. When their child was born her husband was depressed and totally unable to work. Ms. Macy found him to be a chronic liar, and when she discovered that he was having an affair with his secretary, she ended the marriage.

The patient felt that her parents had a bad marriage.

They always seemed to dislike each other. Her mother would often tell the patient that she remained in the marriage because of financial fears. She would nag the patient's father. Moreover, she shared with Ms. Macy that she was discontented sexually with her husband. The patient remembered interceding often to protect her mother from her father's physical abuse. He would push her mother or throw a glass of water at her.

Her father had an explosive temper. He would verbally abuse the patient's younger brother. He would disparagingly call him the "moleman" because he preferred quiet, cerebral hobbies, not athletics, defined by the father as truly "masculine." Ironically, her brother is now a professional weightlifter, a personal trainer. Her father, on the other hand, is overweight. He believed that he was the "brightest man on earth" and could do anything better than anyone else. His friends, though, seemed to like him a lot and he could be the life of the party.

As a child the patient was afraid of her father. He once hit her when she was an adolescent. Oddly enough, her mother had initially provoked her father. This seemed to be a pattern. Her mother would subtly cause the father to be angry and he would take his anger out on the children. Her mother felt inadequate and believed she could not end the marriage because no one would be interested in her. The patient believes that her mother provoked her father to be angry at the patient as a way of gaining his approval. Her father would boast that the patient was brilliant.

Her brother would threaten suicide to manipulate the family.

Ms. Macy's family was filled with conflict and anger. Her father seemed to be the most powerful and intimidating family member. Her mother played a more devious role, pitting the patient's father against the patient. Nonetheless both the patient and her father appeared drawn to each other even as they fought.

From the paranoid-schizoid position, the patient would be drawn to idealized, powerful men, and subsequently would be disappointed in them, or she would choose passive, insecure men and hope to build them into the idealized father. Employing introjection in relation to the man, she could then have a grandiose and persecuting piece of the man come back to her. She also would be prone to devaluate and be critical of others. She would project into the therapist an idealized, sweet understanding aspect of herself, and perceive the therapist as sensitive and empathic, later seeing him as weak and ineffectual. Envy of the therapist may be pronounced and his potency challenged and devaluated since idealization is most frequently followed by envy of the idealized object.

Essentially the patient's ego was split along the following lines: a devious, manipulative self versus a weak, ineffectual self; a grandiose, confident self versus an insecure, anxious self; and an active, alive self versus a lifeless, depressed self.

I would need to watch the following countertransferences: (1) the need to be the idealized, powerful "know-it-all," (2) the insecure, timid, manipulating self, and (3) the depressed, fatigued self, requiring protection.

Another example of an initial session is the following. I shall first present the session as it occurred, and then discuss the dynamics from a Kleinian perspective. It might prove interesting and useful for the reader to speculate about the dynamics from the vantage point of other psychoanalytic models.

The patient, Ms. Wagner, 35 years old, a nurse, attractive and intelligent, began the session not certain as to why she was seeing me. I learned that she had been seeing a psychotherapist off and on for the past two years. She stopped because she was picking up signals that the therapist wanted more than a professional relationship. He would indicate, for example, that he was unhappily married and that he was going to end his marriage soon. The patient felt that the therapist was saying, more than indirectly, "Let's go to bed."

When she began her previous therapy, Ms. Wagner had just painfully ended an affair with her employer. She recalled that two weeks into her employment, he had proposed marriage. She accepted and then he changed his mind, telling her that he could not leave his marriage because of his daughter. Quite depressed, she left the job at this point and moved to another state, where she lived for a year.

Her background is as follows: Her mother, in her seventies, lives in Florida. Her father died when she was 11. He had been an alcoholic who would become violent when he became inebriated. She has two married brothers, one older, the other younger than she. Ms. Wagner has a relationship only with the older brother. The younger one is too much like her father.

She feels close to her mother. Although she has friends, she does not really feel close to them. She will share some things with them, but keeps back significant feelings and experiences. They probably feel she shares deeply with them but she knows better.

The patient views herself as a very keen observer of behavior and prides herself on being able to avoid any contact with someone as soon as she detects any propensity to hurt her. She knows that she is currently depressed, but knows also that she has been depressed before and was able to successfully deal with the problem.

Ms. Wagner has resumed therapy partly because her mother suggested that she do so, and partly because she believes she can no longer continue to run away from her recurring bouts of depression. She also wants to know why she runs away from relationships and does not actively seek out intimacy with a man. She is a believer, though, in fate. If it is meant to be that the right man for her will come along, then it will probably happen without any undue effort on her part. She is ambitious and wants to make more money and, in general, move ahead in her career, buy a house, and perhaps learn interior decorating as a hobby.

The patient appeared both relaxed and seductive with me. I say "relaxed" because she spoke easily and in an organized way. I say "seductive" because she periodically stretched in a slow, teasing manner, displaying her cleavage. She apparently felt quite comfortable acting the part of the *femme fatale*.

Dealing with the session from a Kleinian viewpoint, I find Ms. Wagner to be more in the paranoid-schizoid position at this moment than the depressive position. First, she is uncertain as to why she is initiating therapy, an indication that she has trouble accepting responsibility for her behavior. Second, Ms. Wagner is keenly alert and self-protective regarding any possible threat to herself but lacks any awareness of her possibly harmful impact on others. Third, she has no genuine close relationship with anyone other than her mother. This seems to indicate a highly guarded, distrustful attitude. Fourth, the patient is aware that she is "fooling" her friends into believing they are close. There is a sense of guardedness and perhaps a note of superiority—that is, she knows something they do not know. Fifth, she has poor impulse control, accepting the proposal of a married man after only two weeks of knowing him. Sixth, her projective identifications are quite powerful in that both her former therapist and her employer become smitten with her. Seventh, her ego splits are excessive. There is the split between the part of her self that wants to deal with her depression and the part of her self that has been depressed before and, through acting out or manic defensive control, is able to stave off depression. There is the part of her self that initiates therapy and the part of her self that had to be urged by her mother to enter treatment. She stoically believes in fate — possibly an indication of the manic defense of denial.

I do not obtain a clear picture of Ms. Wagner's mother, which leads me to believe that the patient has introjected her mother in a powerfully diffuse way. As I processed my own inner phantasies, feelings, and anxieties, I felt that I really did not know the patient as well as I should, and might be easily and quickly categorized by her as just another rejecting, controlling, hurting male, like her father, former therapist, or employer, and I might not get the chance to work it through. In fact, my hunch of a quick exit from therapy proved correct. Ms. Wagner came for one additional session, a session filled with superficial chatter, then failed to keep her next appointment. My phone calls were never returned. Once again the patient was running away from her depression, employing acting out, splitting, and projective identifications.

As mentioned in a previous section, the patient newly entering therapy has to grapple with two possible predominant anxieties: one from the paranoid-schizoid position, that based on anxiety that the therapist will make him or her crazy, and one from the depressive position, that the therapist will be made crazy by the patient.

The following is an example of the fundamental anxiety at the beginning of therapy.

Mr. Barnes offered the observation to his wife that she was too hard on herself. At first she was confused and denied that she treated herself in any way harshly. Mr. Barnes pursued his observation, "Everytime you make a mistake, for example, you say that you're stupid."

"Well, that's right, when I make a mistake I am stupid." Her face clouded and her eyes filled up with tears.

"Look," I said, "who used to call you stupid when you were a child?" I hoped to discover with this question the nature of her internal persecuting object, no doubt modeled after a significant childhood object.

"My mother. She still does. Just the other day I was making spaghetti and mixed it with peas. She said, 'That's stupid! Who eats spaghetti mixed with peas?' I was so mad."

Her husband broke in, "So what did you say?"

"Nothing," she replied. "What's the use? She's not going to change. I hate her. I wish she would die so I could be free of her. If I were perfect she wouldn't criticize me."

"So you try to be perfect like mother thinks she is to win her approval," I said.

"So what's wrong with trying to be perfect? And anyway I hate mistakes, and I could never please my mother."

"That's right," said her husband, "and you can't please yourself either. You attack yourself like your mother attacks you."

Mrs. Barnes burst into angry tears. "What am I supposed to do?" Change just like that? I can't! I might as well be dead!"

I broke in, "You see, right here, you are doing it, attacking yourself, wanting to be dead."

"Honey," her husband said, "you can confront your mother. I do. She breaks off when I do. She would respect you more."

Mrs. Barnes looked frightened. The session was about to end.

I said gently, "Mrs. Barnes, when you are ready, you will risk letting your mother know that her criticisms hurt you. She will not die, nor will you."

Of course, it would take repeated interpretations to

consolidate within Mrs. Barnes a conviction that her increased assertion would not cause her or her mother to be ✓
destroyed, that is, go crazy. Mrs. Barnes functioned more
within the depressive position and could be concerned about
others. On the other hand, vestiges of the paranoid-schizoid
position were causing her to fear being destroyed by her
mother's retaliatory wrath.

4

The Positions: Paranoid-Schizoid and Depressive

to be persecuted (be driven mad)
or
to persecute (to drive mad/crazy/destroy)

Knowledge of the two fundamental positions, paranoid-schizoid and depressive, will help the clinician understand and interpret the patient's verbal and nonverbal behavior. Sometimes the patient may manifest behavior that is a combination of both positions. I tend to interpret the depressive position indices first, since I have found that patients find them less threatening, thus easier to assimilate. The state of the working alliance needs to be considered. I try to interpret what I judge the patient capable of understanding and using. Resistances are interpreted before content, since the patient will not be able to let in an insight if a resistance is actively working. Of course, how and why the patient resists is just as important as the content.

The following is a clinical example of the value of applying the concept of the paranoid-schizoid position to the patient's material.

Both Mr. and Mrs. Carlton were struggling to repair a marital atmosphere of hurt, mistrust, and anger. In the session Mrs. Carlton accused Mr. Carlton of being negligent of certain financial responsibilities. He defensively accused her of distorting and overreacting. He then went on to detail how he had adequately dealt with the money matter in question. It seemed clear that Mr. Carlton had, indeed, competently dealt with the disputed issue. Remembering that Mrs. Carlton, had a mother who had persecuted her by narcissistically abandoning her, I wondered aloud if she had transferred her mother's lack of protection and abandonment to her husband. Mrs. Carlton recalled that her mother never really was there for her, and that was what she also felt about her husband. Mrs. Carlton also admitted that she had been feeling particularly vulnerable of late because of two circumstances. In one, a close friend had tactlessly provoked fear in Mrs. Carlton concerning her own health, and in another, her career goals appeared threatened.

I observed that when Mrs. Carlton felt particularly anxious, persecuted, and vulnerable, she projected her rejecting, self-centered mother into her husband and experienced him as an unconcerned, nonprotective persecutor. Mrs. Carlton seemed lost in thought for a moment, then soberly said, "I thought I had a handle on being able to cope with my anxiety, but I guess I don't."

She wanted a husband who would be an idealized protector (an antidote to her mother) and, of course, her husband could not fulfill her wish. Excessive idealization and projective identification followed by anger is one main element in the paranoid-schizoid organization.

Here is another example. Mr. Zahn felt that his girlfriend was passive and had a good deal of difficulty asserting herself and confronting anyone who hurt her. Despite his repeated urging that she speak up and not allow others to hurt her, she continued to remain passive and self-defeating. Conflicted, Mr. Zahn wanted to end the relationship but felt guilty about abandoning his girlfriend, who had stood by him loyally during his own times of turmoil. In a telephone conversation with his girlfriend he scolded and directed her to confront a particularly obnoxious, self-centered, thoughtless friend who had taken advantage of her. His girlfriend cried and they ended the conversation. That same night the girlfriend called to say that she had indeed expressed her anger, and it was clear to me that she craved approval from the patient.

As Mr. Zahn related their conversation it seemed to me that he was still maintaining his resentment and displayed a lack of concern for his girlfriend's poignant efforts to please him and correct her passivity.

His difficulty feeling compassion and sympathy for his girlfriend is typical of the lack of concern for an external object that is associated with the paranoid-schizoid position. The patient was projecting into his girlfriend the split-off part of his passive self. He could feel superior to her and and at the same time continue to punish her for not confirming his potency because of her passivity.

Another example follows of the paranoid-schizoid position as it was manifested through the patient's behavior.

The father of Mr. Juliano, age 58, had been a terribly destructive, controlling autocrat. He would arrange to place his son in a union job, then see to it, since he was the union head, that his son could not make any independent decisions on his job. Since the jobs he placed the patient in were quite lucrative, the patient had allowed himself to be placed in a submissive, demeaning position vis-à-vis his father. When his father died the patient lost his job, and because he lacked any real marketable skills, he was unable to hold on to a job for any reasonable length of time. Adding to his work problems was his ingrained anxiety about becoming an independent adult and about working for someone who, he believed, would be like his oppressive father.

In therapy Mr. Juliano had been able to work out his conflict around other issues, such as intimacy. For instance, he was finally able to marry a devoted, loving, nondemanding woman. However, he was presently unemployed and felt terribly guilt-ridden over his economic dependency on his wife.

During the session he raged against his wife because she had broached the subject of money. She had inquired whether he had ever filed for a pension from a past employment. Her question triggered his guilt and anger at her since it meant to him that she was disappointed in him as a man and as a husband. It also meant that his wife would now launch a merciless campaign for him to obtain a job.

"There are no jobs!" he screamed. "Doesn't she know it?"

I tried to intervene at this point but the patient was too rageful to hear me.

"I've got to leave her! I would rather be alone with the

pain of not working than have to see the pain I'm causing her. She's just like all the other women. When you don't work you're nothing."

I attempted to help the patient see more of the totality of his wife.

"Mr. Juliano, she did not marry you for your money, and she certainly has stuck by you through a lot of set-backs."

The patient was not ready to be reached. "You'll see this is just the beginning. My wife said, 'I'm only telling you that work is good for you.' Right, as if I don't know that. But where is there a job? Show me! I'll work now."

His voice broke with a muffled sob. I was feeling irritated. I wanted to shout at him, "Grow up! Be a man instead of an angry, sniveling child." Instead I said, "You feel like you are not grown up. A voice in you shouts at you, 'You big baby. You will never be the man I am!' "

He stopped. "My father did not want me to grow up to be a man. He had to be the only big shot."

"Do you feel that your wife is putting you down like your father, or exposing the fact that you don't feel man enough like your father said?"

His voice softened. "My wife really cares about me, loves me. She meant well. She just didn't know how awful I feel about not working."

The patient went from the paranoid-schizoid position, where he felt enraged and persecuted by his demanding wife as a surrogate father, to the depressive position, where he could re-experience the totality of his wife. He could now see her as loving and concerned.

I had made a transference interpretation to Mr. Juliano equating his wife with his father, and I had used his projective identification into me to identify and interpret how strongly he had introjected his demanding, persecuting father.

CAN YOU GIVE AN EXAMPLE OF THE PARANOID-SCHIZOID POSITION LEADING TO EXCESSIVE PROJECTIVE IDENTIFICATION?

Vignette: Mr. Yorek, a 30-year-old man, concerned about his failing marriage, his weight, and a chronic depression, began the session by stating that he had been thinking of suicide of late. He was worried about his health and wondered if he had a fatal disease. He pessimistically expected that losing weight and becoming healthier would inevitably be followed by a fatal illness like cancer.

"Look at my father. He died and he was a 'superman,' in great condition."

"So you feel that becoming better causes bad things to happen to you."

"That's the way it was when I was young," he said. "My mother, not knowing what she was saying, said that I was so good as a child they forgot I was there."

"Yes, and that's why they discounted you, made you invisible. The reward for being good in your family was punishment and parents who became dead to you."

The patient's conviction that he would inevitably be destroyed by fate if he became better was his projection of the bad parts put into him by his parents when he was well-behaved or "good." He also expected his wife to desert him when he lost weight, just as his parents abandoned him as a child.

HOW DOES THE PARANOID-SCHIZOID POSITION RELATE TO FETISHISTIC BEHAVIOR?

Vignette: Mr. Ganz, a 50-year-old chemist, entered therapy because he was depressed, lonely, and very bitter toward his wife and daughter. Life was empty and he felt that his future would be filled with further emptiness and hopelessness. He would sit at home and drink as he brooded over what appeared to be his daughter's lack of love for him and his wife's self-centeredness. He believed that his wife wanted him merely as an "escort," and his daughter only wanted his money.

The patient was mired in so much bitterness that his face was deeply lined in a perpetual scowl. He remarked that others were frequently asking him if he was depressed or angry when he only sensed his bitterness toward and not his anger with others. He was also puzzled that friends would flare up at him after what appeared to him to be a rather harmless comment. He wondered why everyone frequently misunderstood his "good" intentions and thought him hurtful, arrogant, and vindictive.

Once therapy began, Mr. Ganz revealed a central, repetitive, disturbing sexual phantasy and compulsion. He cherished and would pursue women with certain specifically shaped breasts, in the present instance breasts belonging to his wife's unmarried sister. Although married, the patient had periodically persuaded his sister-in-law to allow him to fondle and suck her breasts. At those times he would masturbate and experience the "heights of sexual ecstasy" as well as shamed torment. He recalled that when he saw what he considered beautiful breasts, he would spend every waking moment tensely thinking about fondling and kissing them. His mother's breasts, he remembered, were particularly shapely. He also recalled that his older brother had been his mother's favorite. His brother, he believed, had siphoned off nourishment that could have gone to him. He had little emotional connection to his brother now.

Mr. Ganz's mother had died when he was 10. He felt guilty about her death, believing that if he had taken a firmer, more protective position on behalf of her toward his father, she would not have died so young. His father had verbally abused her and, in general, had treated her callously. In fact, his father would verbally punish her severely when she attempted to protect the patient as a child from his wrath.

I shall present two dreams from treatment that I believe illustrate central aspects of Mr. Ganz's phantasy world and his fetishistic relationship to an idealized object, the maternal breast/mommy, persecuting as well as nourishing.

Since the patient's mother died, he had the following repetitive dream. He would see a wolf under a bush or slinking alone through the woods. He identified the wolf as himself, lonely and afraid.

His associations to "wolf" in his dream were ferocious, attacking, and predatory, a hunter and the hunted. He thought of Romulus and Remus suckling at the the teats of the mother wolf.

Mr. Ganz experienced the world as an attacking wolf, having introjected his attacking father. But he was also the guilt-ridden little boy, lonely and afraid of his attacking, brutal, wolfish father. He experienced his father, the carnivorous penis, as possessing the idealized breast that had been forever denied to him.

Melanie Klein (1952a) postulated, based on her clinical observations, that the introjected good, nourishing breast during the paranoid-schizoid position is the basis for the formation of the ego and a fundamental source of reliable internal soothing.

The patient desperately wanted soothing and could only relate to a woman as a good breast, a part-object. He was filled with yearning and anger because his idealized breast/ mommy did not protect him enough from his father. He compulsively searched for the envied, idealized breast and because of splitting, devalued all other women, specifically, his wife and daughter. In subsequent sessions a series of interpretations conveyed all the preceding dynamics. However, he was not able to accept the enormity of his anger and its terrible consequences in all his significant relationships.

When Mr. Ganz dreamed the following, he could not run away anymore from his sadism that originated from his introjected wolfish penis-father.

> I dreamt that I electrocuted the porter, a tall man. I applied electrodes by hand while he was on a hospital stretcher. He did not utter a sound. I applied the electrodes several times and watched the pallor set in. I was vaguely aware that someone was alongside me.

The patient associated to the total dream. He remembered how much he had been exploited and beaten down by his uncles, his father's brothers. They had used him as a porter and paid him very little. He was taken aback by the degree of sadism expressed in his dream. The evidence of sadism in his dream was irrefutable, and we could then begin the necessary interpretation of the split between his rageful, sadistic self and the beaten-down, tormented self. Based on Mr. Ganz's associations to the person alongside him in the dream, he realized that I and the healthy part of his self were that person he vaguely experienced. From the vantage point of the depressive position, his increased acceptance of responsibility, we could now have the opportunity to help him control his split-off sadistic-father introject. We could also obtain greater awareness of the totality of himself, his wife, and his daughter, diminish his envy and compulsive pursuit of the idealized breast, and engage in the necessary repair of his difficult relationships with his family and friends.

CAN A PATIENT MANIFEST BOTH THE PARANOID-SCHIZOID POSITION AND THE DEPRESSIVE POSITION?

Vignette: Having been left enough money to remain comfortably unemployed for the rest of his life, Mr. Deutsch, 34 years old, entered therapy because of guilt over his leisure-filled days and his inability to make any lasting commitment to a woman. His splitting was between a part of the self that wanted to work and be productive and another aspect of his self that considered work a risky, failure-producing undertaking.

When Mr. Deutsch was a child, his father, a hard-driving, extremely successful businessman, had for a long time defined the patient as inadequate and ill-equipped to cope with life's challenges. The father died at a young age and unfortunately Mr. Deutsch's mother never really acted as a counterweight to the father's castration of the patient.

He felt at times that he could be as successful as his father, but he became paralyzed at the thought that he could fail and bring others who would depend on him into financial ruin.

Mr. Deutsch's excessive concern and anxiety for the welfare of others stemmed from the depressive position, whereas his conviction that he could fail originated from the paranoid-schizoid position. He was projecting into the world his persecutory idealized father. Thus he expected that fate would cause him to fail in accordance with his father's predictions.

During therapy on a once-per-week basis, he gradually lessened his idealization of his father and the omnipotent sadistic power that came with the idealization. He reduced the split between his healthy, capable, wanting self and the self that was fearful, and he initiated a successful business undertaking. He also risked a commitment to a woman, subsequently marrying her. Finally, he was able to obtain respect from his mother and siblings, who had shared his father's poor opinion of him, for his business acumen.

CAN A THERAPIST EXPERIENCE THE PASSAGE FROM THE PARANOID-SCHIZOID POSITION TO THE DEPRESSIVE POSITION IN ONE SESSION?

Vignette: Having two older brothers who were intellectually gifted both angered and evoked envy of them in Mr. Kirsch. It was especially hurtful when the patient's father played a passive role in the family. Mr. Kirsch yearned for parental guidance and a validation of his worth, but none was forthcoming. Fortunately, the patient's next oldest brother took him under his wing and, until Mr. Kirsch was the age of 10, this brother encouraged him to use his intellectual abilities as well as pursue other interests to the fullest extent. However, for some inexplicable reason never quite clear to Mr. Kirsch, his brother dropped him at the age of 10 and never returned to the previously cherished intimate relationship. The patient felt the greatest rage toward his brother for this "betrayal."

Mr. Kirsch handled his abandonment by his brother by becoming the undisputed leader of a group of boys considerably younger than himself, then sharply curtailing his association with them later, on the grounds that they were too "young and immature." Thus, the patient turned the tables and did to his younger friends what his brother had done to him.

In Kleinian terms the patient had at first idealized his older brother and had been in turn nourished by him. However, when the older brother had precipitously abandoned him and became the persecuting idealized breast, Mr. Kirsch handled his paranoid anxiety by doing to his younger friends what he felt had been done to him.

In the session the patient admitted that he was feeling anxious and was uncertain as to why. He had just ended a part-time affiliation with a company as a consultant and was very disappointed that his colleagues there had not marked the occasion with a luncheon. He was also worried that he might be discharged from his full-time position, since he was the last one to be hired. This was especially galling since he produced more than any other employee at his level in the company. His girlfriend also disappointed him by not being properly sympathetic to his anxious concerns.

I interpreted that he seemed to be reliving the stressful experience of being dropped by his older brother without explanation or proper justification. Mr. Kirsch's face suddenly reflected deep sadness and he said with a choked voice, "You know what I'm feeling most right now is guilt for the way I dropped my younger friends."

Beginning from the paranoid-schizoid position as the persecuted and the persecutor, the patient was ending the session within the depressive position, able to feel guilt and concern for those little friends he had hurt so deeply in the past.

5

Envy

There are two proverbs that convey the importance of envy
as an affect. They are as follows: "Envy is thin because it
bites but never eats," a Spanish proverb; and from La
Rochefoucauld, "Envy is more implacable than hatred."

These proverbs emphasize the durability and intensity of
envy. It is to the credit of Melanie Klein and her colleagues
that they have focused on envy in their descriptions of
treatment and brought to our attention the many subtle and

sometimes disastrous consequences that occur when envy is not properly monitored by the analyst.

Melanie Klein's (1957) original papers on envy are in *Envy and Gratitude*. She was the first analyst to recognize the significance of envy, and her followers have elaborated upon the impact of envy in many diverse clinical situations.

Rosenfeld (1987), for instance, stresses that the analysis of envy is vital to the working through of the narcissistic omnipotent organization linked to the Negative Therapeutic Reaction. Envy coats the Negative Therapeutic Reaction (NTR) with a patina that destroys therapeutic success, that is, envy is the main ingredient of the NTR, and the main surrounding shell. Rosenfeld advises that the therapist pay special attention to projective, seductive idealizations (disguised narcissistic organizations) in the patient's material.

If, as Klein (1957) postulates, we have received enough emotional nourishment from the good mommy/breast as infants, we develop as adults a conviction of hope, patience, and generosity, and a belief in the basic goodness of those around us. Fundamentally we carry within us a good mommy/breast that loves and protects us and is loved and protected by us.

Infancy is synonymous with intense emotional and physical dependency. In a sense, life from birth and through the paranoid-schizoid position may be seen as one big breast that if present, not present, or present too much or too late, may engender envy and greed. Envy is generated because the infant is enraged when not nourished properly. In effect, the infant may feel persecuted by the bad breast, which omnipotently holds all the nourishment, or the infant may also envy the idealized breast/mommy, which omnipotently retains all the nourishment. The infant may envy the breast/mommy's power. I suspect the reader may think, "My God, this is all so sophisticated! How could an infant have such a complicated inner world?!" There is, of course, no absolute means of proving the existence of Klein's postulated inner world, but I believe that any clinician willing to understand his adult patient's dynamics from a Kleinian perspective will gain new and valuable understanding.

To continue the description of the Kleinian model's understanding of development, the patient reaching adulthood who has been inadequately nourished emotionally as an infant may express intense envy through spoiling, that is, griping about the nourishment not being good enough, anger, and uncertainty about the goodness of others. Envy and greed may be reflected in the patient's wish to devour the therapist or the patient's worry that the therapist will devour him.

CAN YOU PRESENT SOME MORE INSTANCES OF HOW ENVY IS MANIFESTED?

Vignette: Envy.

After a year of therapy, during which time Mrs. Underwood had not manifested the following behavior, much to my surprise I saw her sitting in the waiting room long after her session had ended. She had entered therapy to cope with increasing depression and a curious lethargy that had no organic basis. Her infancy had presumably been uneventful, supposedly with a loving mother and father, but as we continued to work together it seemed that the patient's mother had been mechanically but not emotionally present. Her father, a prominent, strikingly impressive man in terms of looks and career attainment, ran the household with an iron fist and an accountant's ledger. The patient witnessed her father frequently abusing her older brothers physically and compelling her mother to scurry about him in abject, yet worshipful solicitude. Her mother was in awe of the patient's father's charisma and striking eloquence.

As each session ended, the patient, filled with unaccustomed emotional nourishment via understanding and appreciation of her anguish, felt compelled, through envy of me as the good mommy/breast, to stay close to me. As long as she was in the waiting room near me, she could feel more secure and trusting of the nourishment she had received and more certain that she had not destroyed me through her transference envy of my potency.

Here is another example of the role of envy. Mrs. Archer, a 55-year-old divorced woman, had ended her marriage more than twenty-five years ago. Nonetheless, she continued to battle her ex-husband in family court for money rightly owed her, more in the service of getting even with him than out of genuine financial need. What frustrated her and fed her chronic bitterness was the fact that although she inevitably won in court, her ex-husband, through adept legal maneuvering, was able to avoid or delay payment. Furthermore, unlike Mrs. Archer, he was a lawyer and had no legal fees to pay.

Feeling lonely, depressed and bitter, the patient entered once-per-week therapy where from the outset she proved to be a formidable patient. I was berated for being slow-witted, patronizing, inept, cliché-ridden, and, in general, incompetent. These vitriolic assessments were flung at me passionately, without any ambivalence. There were moments when I had thoughts of cheerfully shaking some sense into her and other moments when I longed for the serenity of the creative life of an artist blissfully alone in his studio.

As treatment continued I transferentially became a

well-meaning but bumbling young man earnestly trying to help her, an unsophisticated professional who was not realistic, and finally a kind, frequently understanding, insightful professional from whom she could gain insight and growth.

There were, of course, still intense moments when Mrs. Archer's rage and envy would flare up explosively. The magnitude of her envy and its analysis became a central element of therapy. Among her many envies, Mrs. Archer envied her two young daughters' growth and beauty, she envied her sister's wealth, she envied a friend's recent remarriage, and, finally, she envied my capacity to give appropriately to her through valid interpretations. I was able to interpret a clear instance of the destructive consequence of envy when Mrs. Archer, crying in one session, flung a tissue box at me as I handed her a tissue. She subsequently disclosed that she hated being given something unless she controlled the giving. My solicitous offer meant that I was putting back into her a weak and needy self that she had projected into me for safekeeping. Her envious rage at my supposed strength compelled her to explosively destroy any concern offered to her. Mrs. Archer indicated that for her the optimal relationship with a man would be one in which she could put him in a box and take him out when she needed him. I, unlike the man in the box, gave her a tissue — one *out* of a box — without first obtaining permission from her to do such thing. I therefore incensed her by challenging her powerful phantasy of expedient control over men with this act.

Here is another vignette depicting an aspect of envy.

When younger, Mrs. Xenios was bulimic, but she was now more in control of her eating through constant discipline. She was active and ambitious in her profession. Her husband, more laid back in his work, approached his career without his wife's driven quality. She was angry and disappointed with him. She felt that he should be further along in his profession. As she put it, "He's much brighter than I am."

In marital therapy Mrs. Xenios volunteered that she was envious of her husband's body. He had the discipline to keep his body trim, which she lacked. He worked out regularly and adhered closely to a healthy diet. Her envy of his physical attainment caused her to begrudge him any brief time spent exercising. Faced with his wife's constant complaints that he was taking time away from his family, Mr. Xenios resentfully cut back his daily physical regimen. Mrs. Xenios's envious spoiling of her husband's pleasurable leisure-time activity lessened her envy of her husband's attractive physique. However, marital conflict still remained. As the patient's envy lessened through repeated interpretations, it became possible for her to join her husband in exercise and simultaneously communicate with him while they worked out. Reduced envy helped Mrs. Xenios repair her marriage.

CAN YOU ILLUSTRATE THE RELATIONSHIP BETWEEN SPOILING AND ENVY?

The tendency to spoil any good received or created stems from the corrosive power of envy originating within the paranoid-schizoid position. When the infant recognizes its vulnerable, envious dependency on the idealized breast/mommy, the infant becomes enraged and seeks to destroy what appears to him to be the main source of deprivation, the idealized breast/mommy. The infant does this through biting and clawing.

Later, as an adult, the patient feels envious of the therapist or any good, and will seek to destroy the good through disdain, contempt, cynicism, or pessimism. Here is an example.

Ms. Valenti had been after me to increase her hours. The gap between sessions, she felt, was too long. I agreed with her but could not immediately clear my schedule to meet her request. Finally, a day arrived when I could give her more sessions. The patient's first reaction, surprisingly, was, "Oh, I don't know. I just figured out my budget and that's an extra $200." I pointed out that Ms. Valenti had strenuously pushed for more sessions and that her present response contradicted her former eagerness for additional sessions. This led the patient to indicate that she always felt disappointed whenever she got what she wanted. People and situations inevitably became boring and unexciting.

I asked her if she perceived me as boring. She expected, rather, that I would ultimately be bored with her. Relationships in general were unrewarding. People were so lacking in consideration. Her policy was to drop a friend if he or she hurt her just once. She realized that this was self-destructive. She had dropped many friends without giving them a chance to modify their behavior.

I saw the patient as envious of my power to grant either more or fewer sessions. Her envy caused her to want revenge for my initial inability to quickly grant her wish for an extra session. She felt persecuted by me. When I offered her the additional session, she could project into me her resentment and disappointment. I would now know how it felt to have a need turned down.

I interpreted the preceding thoughts to her and the patient related how she had always been simultaneously angry and envious of her parents' power and rigidity with her. "They never compromised." Ms. Valenti was spoiling my granting of the additional session by relating to me as if I were her rigid, powerful, uncompromising, and spoiling parents.

HOW DOES INTROJECTION RELATE TO ENVY?

Vignette: Mrs. Denton, the patient, was hurt when her sister, who lived in Texas, did not come home for her 40th birthday. But her sister's failure to give to Mrs. Denton was part of a continuing series of disappointments. The sisters were so different. Mrs. Denton was responsible, ambitious, and disciplined. Her sister was divorced, promiscuous, erratically employed, drifting, and unambitious.

In the session Mrs. Denton voiced her anger.

"She's hanging around with our half brother. He hasn't been part of our lives. He and his wife mean nothing to me."

"What are they like?" I asked.

"They're good people. He treats my sister well. In fact I'm relieved that they're there for her. They are possibly the only 'together' people around her."

"So why don't you feel more affection for your half brother?" I continued.

"Look, I know I'm rigid. I also don't want to hurt my father. He's angry at his ex-wife, and I suppose felt hurt by my brother who didn't contact him from the time he was 17 until he was an adult."

I pushed. "Do you think there's more to it?"

"Yes," she said. "My father is impatient and rigid and will quickly detach if he doesn't get his way."

"Does that sound familiar?" I asked.

Pause. "Sounds like me."

Mrs. Denton has introjected her father's traits. However, what is not so obvious is that she is envious of her sister's capacity to charm men and enjoy a relationship with a brother. In subsequent sessions, her envy of her sister's ability to seduce men, to enjoy sex, and to engage in risk emerged and was worked through in therapy. Mrs. Denton was at times angry with me for defining her envy, but she was sufficiently within the depressive position to want to see the totality of her relationship with her ambivalently loved sister. She also wanted to rid herself of her rigidity.

Her initial anger at me for challenging her rigid stance was transferentially based on her seeing me as her critical, rigid, attacking, bad self, which she had projected into me. She wanted me to condemn her sister for not being faithful to her father's wishes and for separating from her.

Mrs. Denton had split her ego in a number of ways, and this also had to be interpreted as follows: the self that was impatient versus the self that was tolerant, the self that wanted a caring brother versus the self that was cut off from her yearning for an affectionate brother, and the self that prided itself on disciplined control versus the self that wanted to be joyfully flexible and free.

CAN YOU GIVE AN EXAMPLE OF THE INTERPRETATION OF ENVY AS A DEFENSE?

Vignette: Mrs. Yaeger, 35 years of age, came from a large family. She had four older brothers and one younger brother. As the only girl, she had to endure being relegated to a second-class citizenship in her family.

She thought of herself as immature and would not deal with responsibility. Twelve years ago, the patient had lived in her parents' home with her out-of-wedlock baby girl for a year and it had been hellish. Her father had verbally abused her and scolded her for "wrecking her life." She subsequently obtained a job and met her present husband there. They have been married ten years and have two daughters along with the out-of-wedlock daughter.

The patient began therapy because of depression and marital problems. She and her husband bicker constantly. She sees her husband as perfectionistic, rigid, and impossible to please. She recognizes ruefully that she seems to have married someone just like her father.

In the session Mrs. Yaeger admitted that she does not believe that she is bright and that her only asset is that she has always been very good in bed. This statement showed me that the patient was in the paranoid-schizoid position, not seeing the totality of herself and persecuting herself as a part-object. I reminded her that she was considered an excellent, competent supervisor at her job. Here, I was attempting to help her move more into the depressive position, toward more awareness of the totality of herself and toward being less self-persecuting. She said that it was hard for her to believe that she was bright, in view of what she was so frequently told by her father and her husband.

She then went on to describe how one brother in her family used her college funds for himself. To me it seemed that she was saying, "If I aspire to a good, my family, someone who is envious and greedy will take it from me and spoil it." I said that she kept herself down, bad, or stupid to defend against her family's rivalrous, spoiling envy. She was also transferentially perceiving her husband as a potentially envious spoiler, when he was in reality encouraging her growth. I had heard the husband urge her to go on for further education and praise her intelligence and abilities. She was projecting the bad father and brothers into her husband and seeing him as persecuting of her when he really was not. I also interpreted the preceding to her.

HOW DOES THE INTERPRETATION OF SPLITTING LEAD TO THE DELINEATION OF PROJECTIVE IDENTIFICATION AND ENVY?

Vignette: Having a sword of Damocles hanging over his head made Mr. Rae quite naturally tense and on edge. The sword was the imminent possibility that the company that paid him so well would go under. Seeking to deny his financial worries, at first it seemed to him a great idea to have his wife go out to a new real estate development to look at the expensive homes there. He could then savor the pretense of affording a "drop dead" house. However, when she returned and began to tell him how lovely and desirable the area was, the patient turned on her in irritation, much to her bewilderment. As Mr. Rae told me how he lashed out at his wife, he himself appeared bewildered and worried about his seemingly irrational, contradictory behavior. As he put it, "I asked her to go out to look at homes. Why would I then become angry at her? She was only doing what I wanted. She was not pressuring me to buy a house now." I asked him to describe the pressure felt. He answered, "It was as if she was telling me, 'You are a failure. You can't do this for your family.' "

The patient had split his ego along the following lines: a

part of his self that wanted the most expensive material things versus a part of his self that would like to retire to an island like Tahiti, away from any stress, and a part of his self that wanted everything and could not stand having to relinquish anything versus a part of his self that fearfully recognized that he was mortal and therefore limited in what he could attain.

Mr. Rae had projected into his wife the parts of his self that wanted it all without limits and a part of his self that wanted the affluent community and expensive house. When his wife returned and shared her pleasure, he perceived her as putting the good back into him to be spoiled by the bad, that is, the financial insecurity still within him. His defensive splitting was being breached. She became his persecutor and he felt compelled to lash out at her.

Since the patient functioned mainly within the depressive position, he could experience concern for his wife and seek to accept responsibility for his puzzling mistreatment of her.

I pointed out his splitting and manic defense of wanting a quick magical fix as an antidote for his tension. When that failed he attacked his wife. He agreed that he had had a brief moment of frustration that he could not offer his family the best at this time. He did yearn for greater control over his life. He also envied his brother, who has a secure civil service job paying considerably less than the patient's job but providing a very fine pension. He envied his brother's pension that would allow him to go off to a small fishing community should he choose, to a life of leisure and serenity. During previous sessions the patient had reported how much his brother had envied Mr. Rae's athletic ability when they were growing up. Here he was envying his brother's good fortune when he had always thought that he would continued to be envied by his brother. It just was not fair.

CAN YOU PRESENT A FIRST SESSION ILLUSTRATING ENVY AND PROJECTIVE IDENTIFICATION?

"I've got double trouble," said the supervisee. I was not sure what she meant. I waited. "My patient, Ms. Tash, is an identical twin and they both came to the first session."

I asked, "How did they dress?"

"Both alike," she replied.

I had asked my question so quickly to gain some idea of the degree of their psychological separation, and from the supervisee's reply it appeared that the twins were maintaining a strong degree of merger. This element would certainly complicate therapy, especially for the supervisee, a relatively inexperienced therapist.

Ms. Tash was 45 years of age, depressed and obese. Her sister was also obese and depressed. She appeared more "together" than the identified patient, however.

"I knew I had trouble," said the supervisee, "when I asked Ms. Tash what brought her into treatment and her sister answered for her."

The twins lived with their mother, who was divorced, as was Ms. Tash, who had two adolescent children, a 16-year-old boy and a 13-year-old girl. The patient made the initial interview quite trying for the supervisee. She spoke slowly and laboriously as might be expected of one so depressed.

"It was like pulling teeth," said the supervisee. "Her life

is empty and passive. She stays home, eats and watches TV with her sister. They subsist on welfare. The only time she becomes somewhat alive is when she speaks about her recently diagnosed multiple sclerosis. She sounds bitterly envious of her sister who does not have this affliction."

It seemed to me, as I listened to the supervisee's description of her contact with the patient, that Ms. Tash's life had repeated her mother's life — for example, divorce, two children, and welfare assistance. The only difference was that Ms. Tash's children were not twins.

The patient's envy of her sister seemed more a product of her paranoid-schizoid functioning than otherwise, and I suspected that, in accordance with this position, there would be strong factors of greed as well as other elements of the paranoid-schizoid constellation. I shared my hunch with the supervisee and she verified it as follows. "Yes, she wants me to solve her problems quickly and fully. I had the sense I was expected to fill her up and it would never be enough. I also tried to get her to look at what she could do under her own initiative, and she got defensive."

At this point I shared with the supervisee that Ms. Tash, while depressed, was mainly coming from the paranoid-schizoid position and would see at this time any attempt on the part of the therapist to help her accept responsibility for her life as persecutory. What the patient wanted was for the therapist to be a more powerful twin or extended part-object. The supervisee's frustration was being projected into her by Ms. Tash, who was expressing a manic defense, that is, a wish for quick, magical reparation. I cautioned the supervisee to expect, along with envy of her, possible contempt and ridicule.

6

Interpretation

HAVE KLEINIAN ANALYSTS
BEEN CRITICIZED FOR
INTERPRETING WITHOUT
REGARD FOR THE WORKING
ALLIANCE OR PROPER TIMING?

While there have been some Kleinians who fire interpretations rapidly at patients, contemporary Kleinians do not.
Today's Kleinian therapist considers how and for how long
the patient is enduring loneliness, suffering, and vulnerability
to criticism, and, most importantly, the patient's unconscious

views of the therapist's interventions. The Kleinian therapist recognizes that the patient is always trying to communicate his inner world to the therapist. All that is required is that the therapist stay tuned in to the projective identifications reaching him and their fallout within his own internal world.

Speaking of "fallout," Rosenfeld (1971) offers a useful criterion for making an interpretation. If the patient is employing projective identification mainly as a form of communication, an interpretation is possible. However, if the patient manifests projective identification largely for evacuative purposes, the patient will adversely react to an interpretation, seeing it as the therapist trying to put his bad back into him. I spot the evacuative projection by feeling a sense of increasing fullness either in my head or stomach as the patient talks. This fullness is probably caused by the patient filling me up with all the introjects he or she wishes to avoid, to megate understanding and working through.

ARE THERE LIMITS IMPOSED ON THE INTERPRETATIVE PROCESS FOR THE KLEINIAN?

While the Kleinian therapist is encouraged to interpret at his own level of anxiety and the patient's greatest point of anxiety, there always needs to be a consideration of another major factor: the recognition of the main position occupied by the patient at the moment. If the patient is predominantly within the paranoid-schizoid organization, interpretations leveled at the greatest anxiety should be held back until the depressive position gains ascendance.

I look for the presence of depressive position elements that correlate positively with acceptance of an interpretation.

These are as follows: lessened projective identifications, taking responsibility for one's behavior, appropriate concern for self and others, ambivalence, more total view of self and others, reduced idealization of self and others, absence of manic defenses, and a need to repair object relationships.

There are also some healthy components of the paranoid-schizoid position that predispose toward the acceptance of an interpretation. These are the use of criticality and the organizational capacity to sort out the contents of the internal world. Aiding the integrative process is the healthy employment of projective identification that fosters the capacity to empathize with the therapist and others.

Here is a case study of a very difficult, challenging session with the parents of an adolescent male patient, Bruce, handled beautifully, I believe, by an astute supervisee, Dr. Stephen Block. Interpretations were held back for good reasons, as we shall see.

The session really began before the actual appearance of the parents, with a phone call from the 17-year-old patient. We had recently been working on his preparing to go to college and separation from his parents and all the stress that these tasks would entail.

"Look, my parents are coming to see you instead of me. They'll be coming in an hour and I'm letting you know even though they don't want you to know ahead of time."

Having met with them twice before, Dr. Block knew the parents first-hand. He had been having difficulty with these parents' interference in the therapy of their son for quite some time, so in one sense he was not surprised that they would not give him the courtesy of prior notification. He suspected that they were coming to sabotage or destroy therapy. He certainly appreciated the patient's call, and was touched and grateful for trying to be protective of him. The patient continued:

"They keep saying, 'Shouldn't you go to see a behaviorist? He'll make you better faster.' "

Dr. Block asked, "What if they're serious and pull you out of treatment?"

"I would be unhappy and I'd let them know it," he replied firmly.

A half hour before the session, the patient's mother called. She informed Dr. Block that she had been given an incorrect bill. She asked if she could rip up the bill. She seemed to imply by her tone that this mistake of Dr. Block's was further proof of his obvious incompetence.

Dr. Block was affected by the two phone calls. He remembered that he had had the fantasy that he wanted to burn the parents by soaking them with kerosene and lighting a match. He then vowed that he would work to understand what was going to occur. He also vowed that he would do what he could to prevent the destruction of the ongoing, so-far successful therapy. He would not be combative, knowing that the parents would not accept any responsibility for their son's problems.

Dr. Block strongly suspected that the patient's parents were both coming to interrogate him in an accusatory fashion. As they entered the waiting room, the father looked more bizarre to Dr. Block than when he had met with him and his wife twice before. He stared at the therapist and sat in a fixed, intimidating posture. The mother wore a stony-faced expression and looked ready to pounce on Dr. Block.

The father greeted Dr. Block with, "We've come to find out about our son's progress."

Dr. Block greeted them pleasantly and invited them into his office. Bruce's mother clutched a small pad. She obviously intended to take notes. With a faint smirk, the mother began the interrogation.

"So how's he doing?"

"He's doing fine."

"Really?"

Both parents then launched into a litany of criticisms of their son and Dr. Block.

Unperturbed, Dr. Block went over their son's progress, listing all his gains since he began treatment, for example, obtained driver's license, did not fall apart (he had made several suicidal threats to his parents when he was very worried that he would not graduate and be able to leave home), got into the college of his choice, and so on.

All this was received with a begrudging, "Yeah, but he's got no friends. He doesn't talk to us and he locks himself in his room every night. He doesn't come out. What should we do about it?"

"I don't think we should do anything," replied Dr. Block. "There is a lot going on. He's got to get through school. He needs space and time. I would not make these things a big issue."

The father continued the assault. "How come he doesn't talk to us? How come he talks to you, not me? You're becoming a surrogate father."

Trying to diminish controversy, Dr. Block answered, "How many 17-year-olds talk to their parents freely? He does need somebody to talk to."

Bruce's father snapped back, "I'm not satisfied with that!"

Mr. Block responded gently, "He does feel that you get on his case a lot. It's very hard to open up because he worries about possible criticism. I understand that you're worried, but the communication comes across as criticism. He needs encouragement, support. Did you ever go away to an out-of-town college?"

"No!"

"It's a big move for your son."

"What do I say to him?" the father asked.

"Well, if there are things that are not right, you can say . . ." [Here, Dr. Block offered some examples of empathic, reassuring statements.]

"What about his social life?"

"That's okay. He has some friends. I think you're encouraging him to continue those relationships. You have a good kid." [Although the parents knew their son had some friends, they wanted him to have "tons" of friends.]

"I agree and disagree with you. I want him weaned away from therapy. We brought him here to be independent, not dependent," countered the father.

"What's wrong with being appropriately dependent? It's all right to ask questions and get answers in therapy. He's a teenager looking for understanding of himself."

"I do not want him dependent. Whose idea was it to go for counseling in college? [The suggestion for college counseling had come from Dr. Block. It seemed that Bruce would need continuing support at college.] We want him to be independent."

Dr. Block explained, "At college they have counseling service. He's going away. It may be rough for him."

"He should talk with his friends," said the father.

Dr. Block tried to explain the difference between talking to a friend and talking to a trained mental health professional. This fell on deaf ears.

The father returned to his main concern. "I do not like him calling you and not coming to us."

Dr. Block reassured him, "I also want him to be able to come to you. I encourage him to speak to you."

The father remained unsatisfied.

Again Dr. Block tried, "We talk about him talking to you, but I don't have the power to compel him to talk to you."

"I know I can be difficult. I can be very impatient. I have financial pressures," volunteered the father.

The session was drawing to a close.

"I really feel that you need to wean our son away from therapy," said the father.

"You cannot abruptly take a baby away from a nipple. These are crucial times in his life. Why not have him come for the three months until he goes away to college?" said Dr. Block.

"I don't want him calling you from college every day. The poor kid. I don't think that he'll make it in college."

Dr. Block disagreed. "My goal is that he *will* make it. I do, however, have students call me from time to time when they believe they need to talk to me. They feel helped."

The father again came back to his central theme. "I still don't know why he comes to you rather than to me."

"I have encouraged him to talk to you," pointed out Dr. Block, and recalled for the parents that their son, with Dr. Block's encouragement, had written a beautiful letter expressing gratitude to his father for helping him to pass the driving test."

"Yes!" the father said impatiently. "I got the letter but I still do not want him speaking to you."

"So how would you like to proceed?"

They looked at each other. Silence.

Dr. Block continued, "My recommendation is that I see him for the next three months."

Bruce's mother stood up, saying, "He'll be here next week." The father, standing by the door, said, "I'm not so sure."

In the supervisory session, Dr. Block admitted that he had been quite drained by this encounter with the patient's parents. Not until later in the day, shortly after another patient had expressed gratitude to him for helping her, did he begin to feel better inside.

I told him that I admired his handling of the session. He had had to face formidable parents and he had astutely realized that they were functioning almost exclusively in the paranoid-schizoid position. Interpretations would, therefore, be totally useless.

Bruce's parents manifested black-and-white reasoning, seeing the therapist as a persecutor of both them and their son in spite of their son's significant gains. They did not wish to look at the totality of their son's treatment experience and did not want to accept any responsibility for their son's problems. They displayed the manic defense of control in that they wanted their son to remain in the suffocating prison of their excessive criticality and domination. The parents' permission to go to an out-of-town college was canceled by their deeper conviction that Bruce would probably fail and have to return home. Fueled by envy of their son's growing independence and separation from them under the guise of wanting more progress — for example, they wished he would communicate (i.e., offer them material to criticize and attack) with them more — they devalued his gains and greedily pushed for magical rapid improvement.

Hoping to reach the parents, Dr. Block applied to his patient the metaphor of the baby abruptly plucked from the breast, a trauma comparable to abruptly ending therapy as the parents insisted on doing, but he did not fully realize, I think, how appropriate his analogy was. Bruce's parents indeed held themselves out as the nourishing breast that was being underutilized by their son. They were partially correct but this was for good reasons. It was his way of protecting himself from their poisonous onslaughts. When the father could offer some good, for example, driving instruction, his son clearly showed his healthy qualities and growth and expressed his gratitude. Bruce's parents envied the therapist's potency and wished to destroy it to strengthen their own potency in order to recapture their son and safeguard his continued pathological dependence on them.

The phantasy of Dr. Block's of burning Bruce's parents becomes more understandable, given the intense, persistent, destructive projective identifications put into him by them. By having this fantasy, he was able to gird himself so that he could be a firm container in processing their poisonous projective identifications of devaluation, envy, greed, and contempt. Nonetheless, such were the intensities of their battering placement of bad into Dr. Block that only when another patient subsequently voiced gratitude could he begin the process of soothing himself from within. One can now more certainly appreciate the son's need to avoid communicating with his parents and physically remove himself from their presence. Not mentioned in the session was the fact that when Bruce had begun therapy he was suicidal, painfully obsessive, and anxiously enraged. All these presenting symptoms were now gone thanks to therapy. Dr. Block heroically struggled to preserve therapy a little longer and repeatedly sought to snag some piece of gratitude from the parents, but to no avail. They were not sufficiently within the depressive position where gratitude and concern for others are present. I do not mean to imply that Dr. Block needed their gratitude. However, some manifestation of gratitude would have placed them in the depressive position where they could have more easily been reached.

The session ends on an enigmatic note with the mother seeming to agree that her son would continue therapy but the father still firmly entrenched in the paranoid-schizoid position expressing the rivalrous, envious, destructive potency of ambiguity.

Postscript: Bruce remained in therapy. He strengthened

his ability to separate from his parents and deal better with his own anxiety about failing in college. He is doing well at school.

HOW DOES INTERPRETATION RELATE TO ENVY?

The following vignette illustrates the value of immediacy, the importance of capturing a patient's curiosity, the impact of colorful imagery, and the significance of the Kleinian concept of inner objects and envy.

The patient, Dr. Vance, a young physician, was struggling to separate from a controlling, depressed mother. At one point in the session, he was describing how concerned he was with his need to suffer through procrastination and the persistence of a weight problem.

"I know that I hang on to my disorganization and my weight," said the patient, "but I don't want to give in to my mother. She's always after me to lose weight and be less messy. If I lose weight, this will show my mother that she was right."

I responded with, "I just made an 'airbet.'"

"What's that?"

I continued; "An 'airbet.' That's a bet without any real money attached to it, a bet I made with myself."

I felt I had Dr. Vance's attention. "A bet within me that goes like this: When will you follow up the exposure of the needy part of yourself with the part that is angry and oppositional? And I won. It's almost as if the angry part of you has to have its day in court because it was becoming envious of the attention the hurting part of you was receiving from me."

He smiled, "You know me. I don't want to surrender to her. 'Airbet,' huh. You're right. I don't want to let go of my suffering."

"Yes," I continued, "and now the oppositional part of you is receiving attention from me and you are pleased and no longer envious."

Let me explain what happened here. I first captured the patient's interest with the provocative image, "airbet." The patient was projecting into me the coercive mother, who was concerned with the patient's needy self. My interpretation was both interpsychic and intrapsychic, that is, a transferential delineation of the internal object's envy of another internal object.

WHAT ARE THE CHARACTERISTICS OF RECONSTRUCTION AS A CONSEQUENCE OF INTERPRETATION?

As therapy progresses, the patient's past unfolds again, picking up new details and fresh perspectives. Six months of therapy have passed for Mrs. Quintero, who initially entered therapy for marital problems, and she now sees her father in a new light. She says, almost in amazement, "I thought my father was never depressed. Yet, he was. When Mom separated from him and went away for a year to the West Coast I was 14 and my father locked himself in his room. We didn't go anywhere. He didn't accept any social invitations."

The patient had introjected her depressed father and projected him into every significant man she met. She then

attempted to repair them through a kind of manic reparation. In each case she failed. Not knowing that she had
introjected her depressed father, she vainly searched for a
man, taking a series of lovers who would infuse life into her.
Her manic defensive (i.e., her insatiable reaching out for
lovers) use of denial and her wish for magical repair of the
depressed man (lover) was impaired by her need to confuse
and daze her husband and her present lover. She had been
confused by her father, who, when she was a very small
child, seemed to be such a source of fun. Mrs. Quintero had
split her father into two objects, an idealized "fun" father
versus a weak, lifeless man. She had projected into her
husband, creating marital woes, and lovers, a lifeless man
followed by an idealized man. This confusing sequence of
projective identifications further confused the men, who felt
injured and depressed.

7

Resistance

DO KLEINIANS IGNORE RESISTANCE?

While Kleinians may not refer to resistances as frequently as classical analysts do, they certainly pay attention to the capacity of the patient to use an interpretation. Racker (1974), for instance, a prominent South American Kleinian analyst who contributed greatly to our knowledge of transference–countertransference interaction, counsels analysts to give an interpretation "when the analyst knows what the patient does not know, needs to know, and is capable of knowing" (p. 41). The therapist needs to address with understanding the patient's material at the point of urgency, that is, at that point in the patient's inner world in which the most containable anxiety is evoked.

CAN YOU ELABORATE FURTHER ON HOW KLEINIANS ADHERE TO THE CONCEPT OF RESISTANCE?

Joseph (1989), for example, discusses some aspects of aggression in which the patients are very noticeably constrained in their expression of assertiveness. They seem to want the analyst to carry the main responsibility for change in analysis. These patients have failed to discover who they are.

If the patient accepts and internalizes the interpretations, he fears his success in treatment will lead to destructive envy of him by his therapist. The patient's passivity becomes a defense against envy.

Joseph (1989) postulates splitting that results in two selves, one lifeless and self-sufficient, an observer of treatment, and the other, healthy and desiring positive change. The lifeless, destructive self is committed to destroying therapy through acting out and other resistances. The patient projects into the therapist the healthy self, evoking in the therapist an alive, active desire to understand and reach the patient. While the therapist basically struggles on behalf of the patient, the self-destructive, omnipotent self remains inaccessible. As long as the therapist does not succeed, the patient need not experience envy. Envy is avoided when the patient simultaneously attacks and fragments his capacity for self-observation as well as destroys the therapist's understanding.

WHAT ARE SOME OTHER INSTANCES OF HOW A KLEINIAN LOOKS AT RESISTANCE?

We have all encountered patients who use denial to avoid experiencing suffering. We see this usually as a manifestation of a common defensive mechanism. Joseph (1989), offering new insights, views the avoidance of psychic pain through the Kleinian lens.

According to Joseph, patients avoid psychic pain through a variety of means. They may contain their anxiety through a fetish or a delusional system projected into the analyst. Patients who avoid psychic pain appear to have little concern for what the analyst says and they may continue to complain of a gnawing sense of emptiness. They retreat from pain by partially slipping back to the paranoid-schizoid position. Consequently, they destroy therapeutic progress and parts of the self.

Joseph suggests that the analyst monitor any shift toward the paranoid-schizoid position in the transference that is characterized by a patient's lack of concern for himself and others, a lack of responsibility, and general lack of self-awareness. Monitoring and interpreting the paranoid-schizoid transference may thus lead to a shift toward the depressive position.

The effort to avoid anxiety is at the heart of resistance. Kleinians are most sensitive to the vicissitudes of anxiety and how it combines with projective identification in particular and with the paranoid-schizoid position in general to emerge as resistance (Joseph 1978).

The main task of the Kleinian therapist is to locate the immediate anxiety as manifested transferentially or otherwise, and understand how the patient is resistively attempting to involve the therapist in a collusion, that is, a defense against the anxiety. The patient attempts to use the therapist to obtain misunderstanding instead of liberating insight. Countertransference is the main vehicle by which the therapist gains awareness and understanding of the patient's anxiety and the various mechanisms, for example, projective identification, used to avoid anxiety. Thus patients will resistively exude reasonableness, pseudo-understanding, pseudo-maturity, emptiness, or blandness.

Joseph (1978) suggests that the therapist reach deeply into himself to become aware of the potential interpretation he would like to offer that would evoke the most anxiety in himself. It is precisely at this level or point that the therapist needs to interpret.

HOW DO KLEINIANS DEAL WITH A PATIENT WHO IS DIFFICULT TO REACH?

Joseph (1989), for example, is most aware of the myriad subtle resistances manifested by patients. She also considers the vital contribution countertransference plays in the understanding and working through of intractable resistances.

There are patients who appear unreachable despite what seem to be valid interpretations given at the proper time. These patients may appear to be working hard in therapy but, Joseph (1989) discovered, a part of their personality is actively working to keep a needy, receptive area split off. The consequences are apathy, detachment, or passivity, coinciding with frequent use of projective identification.

Joseph suggests that the analyst concentrate on how the patient communicates rather than on the content. She advises that we need to make contact with that part of the patient's self that wants and needs understanding and not the anti-understanding part.

> # HOW DO YOU MAKE
> # CONTACT WITH THE
> # POTENTIALLY
> # UNDERSTANDING PART?

Concentrating on how the patient communicates sharpens awareness of the anti-understanding part of the self. What also helps is focusing on how the therapist is being used. Sometimes we have to delay interpretations of projective identifications; we need to contain the patient's criticisms. We need to approach interpretatively how the patient uses the therapist's mind. Envy also plays a significant role. The anti-understanding, infantile part of the patient's self destructively nullifies the therapist's interpretations in order to avoid being envious of the therapist's potency. The various nuances of envy need to be monitored and interpreted.

WHAT ELSE CAN YOU SAY ABOUT THE KLEINIAN VIEW OF RESISTANCE?

Fundamental to analysis and dynamic psychotherapy is the element of understanding. We speak not only of the therapist's understanding of the patient, but of the patient's understanding of the therapist. Misunderstanding of the patient may be due to countertransference or merely to incompetence. The patient may also continually misunderstand, based on being predominantly at the paranoid-schizoid position.

The paranoid-schizoid position's defenses and primitive splitting destroy understanding (Joseph 1983). It is only within the depressive position that patients can take responsibility for their selves and relate to the therapist as a total person. By contrast, the patient predominantly in the paranoid-schizoid position excessively uses projective identification, splitting, and omnipotent denial. As a result this material is often flat and sterile.

Joseph (1983) suggests that the therapist seek out that part of the patient's self that is needed for understanding but is not available. The therapist needs to become aware that what has been created is a spurious working alliance. The active, alive, understanding, motivated-to-change part of the patient has been split off and projected transferentially into the therapist. If I feel, for example, that I am becoming more zealous and forceful in my interpretations and the patient seems more and more unable to understand and integrate the interpretation, I know that the patient's healthy self is in me and his passive, inert, unmotivated self is spiraling away and warding off any possibility of my reaching him.

We have usefully reconnected to the patient's healthy self when, through his projective identifications into us, we can regain the alive part of the patient's self in the treatment room.

GIVE AN EXAMPLE OF HOW INTROJECTION AND PROJECTIVE IDENTIFICATION ARE EXPRESSED RESISTIVELY.

Mrs. Raab, in once-per-week therapy, goes back and forth concerning her decision to reconnect once again to her ex-husband. He attracts her through his reliability, sense of responsibility, all-around competence, and steady concern for her welfare. However, the patient does not feel any libidinal excitement. Sex is mechanical. With other men, who are irresponsible and unreliable, Mrs. Raab can experience sexual excitement.

In the session, the patient shared her lifelessness and depression. She once more felt conflicted about going back to her ex-husband. If she remained unmarried, she worried about her future, her being alone and lonely. There would be no children, nothing she had created that would be worthwhile and satisfying. Her work was no longer good enough. I broke in at this point and asked her about her loneliness. Did she ever experience those feelings in the past?

She remembered that as a young girl, 6 or 7 years of age, she had been strongly attached to a female cousin, F., the same age as herself. F. was exceptionally attractive and popular. Mrs. Raab, on the other hand, saw herself as "fat and ugly." On numerous occasions, F. would drop Mrs. Raab and go off with other friends.

During the session, as the patient spoke about her childhood, she felt powerlessness, hurt, loneliness, and anger. She envied her cousin's beauty and popularity. F. was happily married to a wealthy, handsome man and had a wonderful child. The patient expressed her rage, not against F., but against F.'s father, who apparently had not allowed Mrs. Raab's mother to maintain contact with F.'s mother. I wondered to myself why the patient was protecting F. from her anger but freely expressing it against F.'s father. I then remembered that Mrs. Raab's father, working two jobs, was absent for most of her early childhood. He was an exciting, libidinal figure who was there but not there—like the irresponsible men she found so sexually exciting. Mrs. Raab's cousin F. also had been exciting and had abandoned her.

The patient had introjected two selves, exciting and rejecting, modeled after her cousin and father. These two selves persecuted her and she defended against envy of them by maintaining an idealization of them. She kept her lifeless self going by contact with exciting, irresponsible men. In therapy she projected her lifeless self into me, causing me to feel impotent and unable to reach her through interpretations.

GIVE AN EXAMPLE OF THE MANIC DEFENSE EMPLOYED AS A RESISTANCE.

Three years into therapy, Mrs. Landau, 50 years of age, was attempting to understand why she had selected her ex-husband. He turned out to be alcoholic, passive, and irresponsible. After two children, the patient found her marriage intolerable, divorced him, and went back to school to become a competent professional.

The patient's father had been regarded by her mother as a "loser." True, he communicated his feelings and tried hard to tune in to Mrs. Landau's mother, but he did not earn enough money to please the mother and so remained firmly in her mind in the "loser" slot. The patient adored her father, now deceased. Fortunately, aiding the patient in releasing resentment toward her mother on her deathbed was the realization that her mother really had loved her father and that her mother considered herself very lucky to have been married to him.

As a child, the patient had introjected her mother's contempt for her father and largely functioned within the paranoid-schizoid position with regard to men. To preserve an idealized picture of her father, she picked a man totally his opposite. As she put it, "I did not want to replace my father." She split men into two categories: idealized and out of her reach, or contemptible, childlike creatures, who, to her, were the majority of males.

I frequently brought to Mrs. Landau's attention her black-and-white perception of men and her difficulty in seeing a man in a more complex, ambivalent, and total way. Although she made some progress toward perceiving men more from a depressive position rather than from the paranoid-schizoid position, she still has not shaken off the conviction that men cannot be trusted and will ultimately turn on her. When I point to our relationship as the antithesis of what she expects of men, she laughingly says, "How do I know what you would be like as a husband?" My hunch is that the patient is still anxious about replacing her idealized father with me. In addition, she projects her distrust, black-and-white reasoning, and expectation of being ultimately persecuted into men who often elicit the very behavior she fears. Her manic defense of control, denial, and triumph over men has proven a formidable barrier to continued progress in therapy.

CAN YOU CONFRONT THE MANIC DEFENSE OF MAGICAL REPAIR?

When do you push a confrontation and when do you back off? This is an issue all therapists face. Considering when to forcefully confront, of course, is dependent not only on the current dynamics of the patient but on those of the therapist as well. Take a therapist who for physical or emotional reasons is not doing well; he or she would be advised not to confront but to hold off. It is vital to keep negative affects such as anger, frustration, or punitiveness out of the confrontation, since they may give the patient an opportunity to seize on them as reality, to justify his or her running away. Sometimes, though, a patient may need a confrontation, because there are probably not going to be any subsequent sessions. Such was the case with Mr. Madden.

The supervisee, Dr. Stephen Block, a well-trained, sensitive psychologist-psychoanalyst, started our meeting by saying, "Irv, I think I blew it. I feel really bad. I just was not feeling too well. I was thinking about some minor health problem and was not paying full attention to this patient." I asked about the patient.

Mr. Madden is a 22-year-old, handsome, well-built weight-lifting man who had been in therapy with Dr. Block for six months on a once-per-week basis. He had entered therapy complaining of depression and a problem getting along with his parents. He made some progress during the six months of treatment, enrolling as a student at a nearby community college and obtaining a job. He had one long-term relationship (four years) with a girl, which broke up during therapy. Evidently the girl wanted a commitment but the patient would not make one. He claimed that he did not feel as close to her as she did to him. He did see her, however, as his dearest and closest friend. With regard to this girl-friend, he appropriately reasoned that he was setting himself up for trouble. She apparently was taunting him with her relationship with her former boyfriend and this proved too painful for him to accept.

The patient has a very good facade of bravado and charm. Most people who meet him initially think of him as very attractive. However, he considers himself inadequate and a "lightweight."

His first six months of therapy ended against the super-visee's wishes. The patient, himself, admits, a year after his last session, that he ran away from the therapy and had now returned to do the "right thing" which was to say "goodbye" properly.

Dr. Block was, of course, chagrined and disappointed that Mr. Madden had merely returned after a hiatus to establish closure and not to continue needed therapy. During this return session, he felt that everything the patient was saying was a smoke screen. The patient compulsively chat-tered and, as Dr. Block put it, "He talked a blue streak," obviously running away again even as he seemed to be back in therapy.

Some background information: The patient's mother is very close to him, too close. She wants the best for her son, she says. His father is a perfectionist, "Mr. Right," successful in his career. Both parents say they wanted their son repaired so they can get on with their lives. The patient has a great deal of of rage toward his father, who frequently picks on him. When Mr. Madden was 16 or 17 years of age, he and his father actually came to blows.

When the patient graduated high school, he worked for an established catering concern and they thought highly of him. They liked him so much that he was made manager. For a time he toyed with the idea of becoming a chef, but was discouraged by both parents.

The supervisee attempted to point out some problems to the patient in order to foster a commitment to therapy, but Mr. Madden did not prove receptive. He countered with a noncommital response, implying that he would think about resuming therapy, but Dr. Block held out little hope that the patient would return.

I granted that the supervisee was probably right and that no amount or kind of interpretation might have reached the patient and caused him to change his mind. I added that the patient probably believed that by merely seeing the therapist once, he would receive his final stamp of approved termination. The supervisee added that the patient had shown from time to time an impatience and a penchant for magical results. He also related that the patient had a low threshold for pain, although when he was hurt he did not run away but would charge into the scuffle. This characteristic had made him a wonderful football player. I missed this element in my initial understanding of the patient. This insight could, in part, explain why he is afraid of therapy. He could be terrified of destroying the therapist. In other words, he may run away from therapy and from his former girlfriend out of concern for them, a manifestation of the depressive position.

I suggested to the supervisee that he invite the patient in for a session, during which time he might confront the patient with his habit of setting up expectations in others, then disappointing them. I suspected that he projects into others — the therapist, his girlfriend and his friends — an expectation of increasing collaboration, commitment, and closeness, then causes the same disappointment in them that he felt in relation to his father. I urged Dr. Block to forcefully say this to him. Dr. Block hesitated then said, "Irv,

I think he will just respond with, 'I'm doing fine and I don't need any therapy.' " I answered, "Yes, I suppose he might very well say this, but I would then respond with, 'It takes time for you to discover how and why you don't have now a closest and dearest friend. One session will not give you positive results magically.' " With this confrontation I was trying to counter the patient's excessive concern that he could be harmed by the therapist and deal with his manic defensive denial.

In the light of my belated insight, I would add that the supervisee should have informed the patient that he, the therapist, would not fall apart if the patient expressed anger. The confrontation might not work but, I believe, the therapist had everything to gain and nothing to lose. Perhaps Mr. Madden was functioning well enough in the depressive position to experience the supervisee's reassurance that he was a strong container capable of surviving the patient's rage. In other words, the therapist would not run away, although the patient might choose to run away from therapy once more.

HOW DOES A KLEINIAN TREAT AN IMPASSE IN THERAPY?

Rosenfeld (1987), a prominent, pioneering Kleinian, has written extensively about the obstructive forces in analysis. What occurs in analysis that is antitherapeutic also applies to psychotherapy.

What the therapist must do is monitor his unconscious need to avoid anxieties stirred up by the patient. If the therapist is not in touch with his own anxieties, he will collude with an aspect of the patient's inner world to avoid important conflicts, anxieties, split-off noxious internal objects, part-selves, transferences, resistances, defenses, and phantasies. In essence, the therapist must interpret empathically to the patient what he, the therapist, most fears interpreting.

> ## SOME PATIENTS HAVE A PROBLEM DEPENDING TO ANY EXTENT ON THE THERAPIST. HOW DOES THE KLEINIAN VIEW THIS RESISTANCE?

Joseph (1959) has found that dependency-fighting patients anxiously avoid neediness, loving, and prizing of the primary object, the idealized breast. Dependency for them evokes envy, hatred, and ambivalence. The patient splits off the needy, dependent self and projects this self into external objects. The external objects are split still further into a bad, persecuting, greedy self and a self that is both idealized and integrated.

With regard to the therapist, the dependency-avoiding patient projects a part of the self into the therapist and introjects and identifies with the analyst's capabilities. In effect, the patient triumphs over the therapist by taking over the therapist's role. For example:

Ms. Sabatino, a 30-year-old single woman, entered therapy because she had experienced incest but had only vague bodily memories or derivatives of the event. During a number of sessions the patient would suggest various therapeutic techniques (e.g., hypnosis, drawing, sensory exercises, books, etc.), to facilitate her recall of the sexual abuse. Since the therapist could not make it happen, she felt that there should be some technique that could cause her to relive her sexual trauma in all its vivid details. Thus, the therapist became an inept, failing professional, through the patient's projection of parts of her self.

However, when the therapist succeeded from time to time in reaching the patient with an insight, the patient, instead of expressing gratitude, would subsequently intensify her complaints that she was insufficiently being helped. Ms. Sabatino could not abide the therapist's potency and aliveness. With relatives and friends, she also shared how much she was suffering to avoid their possible envy of her.

WHAT IS THE KLEINIAN EXPLANATION FOR THE NEGATIVE THERAPEUTIC REACTION?

Rosenfeld (1987) has tied the Negative Therapeutic Reaction to what he terms a *narcissistic omnipotence structure*. Essentially this narcissistic omnipotent structure has a very primitive superego at its core, sadistically devaluating and belittling the patient's capacity to be concerned and considerate to external objects or to himself. When the patient feels better after a "good" session, this narcissistic omnipotent structure creates guilt and disruptive acting out, for example, coming late, forgetting what happened in the previous session, and so forth. The patient appears to be attached to a split-off, destructive, sadistic self, a self that is viewed as a "glue" holding the patient together. The analyst has to demonstrate convincingly how significant figures in the patient's early childhood made envious attacks on the patient when he triumphed or attained good.

WHAT IS THE KLEINIAN'S GREATEST PRIORITY WHEN IT COMES TO CONNECTING COUNTERTRANSFERENCE TO THE PATIENT'S RESISTANCE?

There are many threads that potentially can be picked up and nourished in a session that would expose the inner phantasy world of a patient. Sometimes the very richness of a session can be overwhelming and confusing. The crucial task becomes essentially one of choosing a priority or, as Kleinians prefer to conceptualize, the point of greatest anxiety or defense both for the patient as well as the analyst.

For example, I will describe what was, at first, a confusing session, and later was less confusing after the session was over.

Dr. Garrity, a mental health professional, began the session by wondering if I could fill in the gap between Erikson and Freud's ideas about religion. I decided to treat his query on a manifest content level and answered that I thought that both saw religion as a projection of man's dependency needs and an idealized parental figure gratifying those needs. He beamed and said, "Exactly. I never thought of that." I felt that I had not uttered a magnificent truth. Why so much gratitude? I felt uneasy and confused.

Dr. Garrity went on to talk about confusion and unrest with regard to his lover. She praised her husband's good qualities even as she extolled the patient's value for her. Dr. Garrity did not believe that his lover really tried to help her husband grow as he had done and continued to do with his own wife. Last weekend, he and his wife had stayed at a nearby hotel and he had had a good time. In the past, his wife had treated him with scorn. This time, he gave her space to do her thing while he did his. Perhaps, he speculated, he could enjoy being with his wife because of the existence of his lover in his life. Toward the end of the session he told the following dream.

> He was in Penn Station with two of his wife's female cousins. They were wearing sunglasses. Dr. Garrity was not, but put on his sunglasses when urged to do so by the cousins.

His associations to Penn Station were that of confusion and unrest, a place in which you go from one place to another. To cousins, he associated blindness. One cousin did not want to see that her father was an alcoholic, while the other cousin denied her sexuality. Wearing sunglasses meant emotional blindness to Dr. Garrity.

I said to the patient that he was confused by his lover, who seemed to show an inability to value a man properly. I indicated that Dr. Garrity wanted to be treated as special but selected both a lover and a wife who did not appear to value him very much.

After the session ended I felt uneasy and confused. I was troubled by the thought that I had missed the boat or had not gotten to what was most essential. I had not considered enough the confusion projected into me by the patient. I had failed to see that the two blind cousins in his dream were really Dr. Garrity, himself. He was running away from properly seeing the two women in his life, his wife and his lover. In addition, I had failed to perceive that his question concerning the gap between Freud and Erikson referred to me. He wished that I would be able to fill in the gap between his wife and his lover. With me he could talk theory and would be special. He wanted to wear "sunglasses" in therapy, so as not to see what was really causing his confusion and his inability to choose between his wife and his lover. I had colluded with him by not interpreting his resistance. I had joined him by also wearing "sunglasses."

My countertransference originated from my paranoid-schizoid position whereby seduced narcissistically, I wanted to be for the patient a masterful idealized analyst, a superior combination of Erikson and Freud. The patient, from the paranoid-schizoid position, wanted an ideal so that both the patient and I in collusion could have gone along for some time doing unproductive work.

Another example follows. Ms. V., the supervisee, was young and inexperienced. This was her internship in a busy, cosmopolitan mental health center with many varied, challenging cases. She began the supervisory session with "Mrs. Radner is a patient whom I presented to my supervisory group a while ago, and I thought that since then everything was going to go well." She faltered. "But I think I goofed and I don't know how to fix it."

"What's the problem?"

"The patient is one of my best. She's 46 years old, a lab assistant at a local college. She's never been married, though she had two long-term relationships, one for two years, the other for five. She came in for depression and loneliness. I think she also has an eating disorder. She binges episodically. I haven't told her that I'm going to leave in three months, and I asked her if she would consider coming for two sessions instead of one per week.

"She agreed. I know that I have problems with intimacy and detachment. I'm working on these problems in my own therapy; I have the same problems as the patient. In one way

I think that our similar problems have helped me help her better. But I think I should not have asked her to commit now to an additional session per week."

"Why?"

"Well, I thought she's such a good patient. She's made progress. She's less depressed, and lonely, and is still in therapy. She will even catch herself resisting and say, 'Uh, oh! I'm running away,' then go back to where she was derailed. But she was also feeling a lot of pain and I felt that more sessions per week would help her get through that pain. A good idea, I thought, but I didn't consider enough what may happen when I tell her I'm going to be gone in three months."

"Tell me more about her background."

"Well, her problem of intimacy and detachment takes the following form: She quickly develops a crush on a man, wants to be close, but is unable to be. She also had Epstein-Barr syndrome with a lot of fatigue when she started therapy. She was out of work for six months. Her mother and sister were of no help to her then and, in fact, turned their backs on her.

"When she first came I thought she was somewhat schizoid. She chose to live on a deserted island by herself for one year and later lived alone in a ghost town for another year. All this was done in her twenties. She loved it.

"I found her elusive at first. That stage passed and now things are going well."

"What about her father?" I had noticed that no mention had been made of him.

"He died when she was in her twenties. He was an emotionally remote man. She doesn't say much about him. It's her mother that she wants to work on. Her mother was a teacher. The patient also is fourteen years older than her married sister, who has two children, a boy, 2, and a girl, 5.

She feels close to the kids and tries to see them at least once a week. Her mother sounds like a sick cookie."

"What do you mean?"

"She would go into silent rages frequently for long periods of time. When the patient would ask her why she was angry with her, she would say, 'If you don't know why, then I'm certainly not going to tell you.' Her mother would give the patient pots and pans to play with when she was a small child and then take them away when the patient was enjoying herself because she was making too much noise. And this is odd — the patient vividly remembers, when she was 4 years old, being in the kitchen on the floor and very deliberately and calmly asking herself, 'Should I love my mother?' "

I realized that the supervisee was feeling guilty and confused — guilty about giving the patient mixed messages, that is, the opportunity to choose more sessions, yet, unbeknownst to the patient, the message of "I'm leaving in three months." The supervisee's departure would no doubt be traumatic and would recreate the patient's childhood experience of being given pots and pans to play with then having them abruptly taken away when she was enjoying herself. I gently shared this thought with the supervisee.

"I know. I know. I thought of that and that's one of the reasons I feel so guilty and feel I goofed."

"What about your not telling her yet that you will be leaving in three months?"

"Another goof, I think."

"You must tell her," I urged. "The patient already has a mother who expected her as a young child to read her mind and punished her for her inability to do so."

The patient's mother was functioning within the paranoid-schizoid position and could not tolerate separation because of her envy of her daughter's enjoyment of life. She also persecuted the patient with chronic rages and used a manic denial of the realistic separation between them; she expected her daughter to read her mind.

Now came the most difficult part in the supervisory hour:

"Look," I said, "it's possible that you countertransferred out of envy of the patient's progress in dealing better with intimacy. You yourself said here that you have problems in that area. That part you can take up in your own therapy, if I'm correct. I believe that you ought to tell her that you made an error in asking her to commit to more sessions without telling her you will be leaving in three months."

The supervisee interrupted, "I'll take up the envy issue in my therapy. I think you're right there, but how do I tell her that I'm leaving in three months now without devastating her?"

"You say, 'I made a mistake.' You then ask her to collaborate with you in determining what she feels and understands about your disclosure of your error. You leave the possibility of extra sessions open."

I suggested to the supervisee that she disclose her error because I wanted the patient to experience the supervisee as coming from the depressive position in contrast to her mother, who had operated mainly from the paranoid-schizoid position. I hoped that the patient would experience the supervisee's concern for her and the treatment process, the effort to repair an error, the acceptance of responsibility, the valuing of the totality of the experience, and respect for the patient. In short, I hoped that the damage that the supervisee's countertransference had caused would be remedied and the supervisee's containing function would be restored.

Money-Kyrle (1956), a Kleinian, has argued that the analyst's confession of an error may be perceived by the patient as his (the patient's) impotence projected into the analyst and confirmed by the confession; this may bring on the patient's contempt. I suspect that the scenario Money-Kyrle describes may indeed occur at times and should be kept in mind by every therapist before he or she exposes an error. I think in the example presented here, the patient's history speaks strongly in favor of candor and a strenuous effort to counter the patient's mother's entitlement to mind reading. I think that the supervisee says with her confession of error, "When one party in psychotherapy does not communicate essentials, issues of vital concern to the other, therapy is in trouble. This condition needs correction." This approach, I believe, demonstrates the supervisee's potency rather than impotence, that is, the safeguarding of reality rather than the preservation of the idealized, omniscient breast/mommy therapist.

WHAT IS AN EXAMPLE OF A PATIENT AT THE DEPRESSIVE POSITION?

All her life Mrs. Egan timidly held back her anger. Her husband, an alcoholic, verbally abused her and placed the family in financial jeopardy. The patient never confronted him. Finally, he ended the marriage and Mrs. Egan struggled to keep her three young children adequately housed and clothed. She obtained a position as a teacher and thus gained a measure of security. However, she remained passive and timid. Her principal was able to exploit her freely, assigning to her the toughest teaching positions. The patient never complained or asserted herself. Her boyfriend, an eccentric retired artist, treated her purely as a means of sexual release, restricting his contact with her to once a week at a nearby motel. Mrs. Egan unquestioningly accepted this.

The patient was mainly in the depressive position, always worrying how she might be hurting others (e.g., ex-husband, boyfriend, principal, and therapist). With me she was self-effacing and ready to apologize quickly if she thought she offended me in any way. The transference was mainly an idealizing one. I was for her the authority, asexual, and unerringly wise. She just could not be angry with me.

The patient's father, the alcoholic, had verbally derogated the patient. Her mother appeared to have been an ineffectual, shadowy figure in the patient's life. Repeatedly her parents adversely compared the patient to her brother, a mathematical genius. In a sense, Mrs. Egan's parents, like her husband and boyfriend, ignored the totality of the patient, her loyalty, devotion, and sense of responsibility.

I had repeatedly to reassure Mrs. Egan that I would not fall apart if she displayed even the mildest irritation with me. I had to understand how she was projecting into me her own sense of being only a part-object, my being a "breast of knowledge" that she could incorporate. When she was able to see me as a man first and as a therapist second, she could take back her projection and begin to become angry with me. Of course I did not fall apart, and the patient could then bring together that part of her self that was excessively guilty and paralyzed with the self that was sturdy and resourceful. In other words, Mrs. Egan could move from the more fragmented paranoid-schizoid position to the more integrated depressive position.

WHAT ARE SOME EXAMPLES OF HOW PROJECTIVE IDENTIFICATION CREATES COUNTERTRANSFERENCE AND THE ACTING-OUT RESISTANCE?

The patient, Ms. Ziegler, had completely stymied the female supervisee. The impasse illustrated a basic truism believed by all therapists of whatever persuasion: "In order for therapy to occur, the patient has to come to the session." This 20-year-old depressed patient would come to some sessions and skip others. To make matters worse, she could not be reached. Every time the supervisee thought she had a phone number, the patient would move, leaving no forwarding number.

After I listened to the mounting frustration of the supervisee for some time, I interrupted her and asked, "What are you feeling?"

"Frustrated, angry, unable to reach her."

"So tell me about her background."

"Her mother was verbally and physically abusive to her. Her mother has been angry with her since the patient had a child when she was 15 years of age. I interpreted that the supervisee's countertransference feelings of impotence and escalating frustration were aspects of the passive, abused part of the patient's self that the patient was projecting into the supervisee. The patient was enacting the role of the abusive, rejecting mother. When the patient showed up at the next session, the supervisee began to interpret the preceding dynamics and the patient's acting out subsequently stopped.

Another example of projective identification's relationship to countertransference and the patient's resistance follows.

"This past week has been very interesting," Mrs. Rabin said at the beginning of the session. "Y. has been really mystifying to me. He told me that he had anticipated that I would hurt him, and then I did, when I wanted him to consider the contradiction he was expressing: saying that his wife was his "life raft" and his desire to have an affair with me."

"Y. doesn't seem able or willing to take a look at himself," I offered.

"Yes, but he then comes and paces back and forth in my office and tells me that as much as he would want me, he thinks we should be good and not go any further with our relationship."

Mrs. Rabin smiled. Her eyes sparkled. "He was pacing back and forth and I felt so much pleasure seeing him do this. I was no longer furious with him."

I asked "Why?," feeling puzzled by her seeming pleasure at seeing Y. so conflicted and distressed.

"Because I enjoyed his wanting me. I felt like something then, not nothing. He had not forgotten me."

I asked her to give me more associations to being wanted and how that turned her on. She went back to early childhood. Apparently her maternal uncle was the only man who indicated clearly that she was desirable. He would recite romantic poetry to her even as he became increasingly inebriated. He may have molested her, although the patient had no conscious memories of sexual abuse. Her father was only interested in her mother and brother. They were needy and her father gave to them, not to the patient. The patient's maternal uncle had moved to South America after his wife died and was seen once a year. The patient's mother, a self-centered, angry woman, ignored the patient.

I interpreted that Mrs. Rabin's strong attraction to Y. was based on the number of buttons within her that Y. could push. I offered the reconstruction that as a child, the patient had identified with her self-centered mother and had, in addition, felt rejected by her father, her maternal uncle, and even her grandfather, who, despite his open fawning over the patient, returned inevitably to his wife. Moreover, the patient had been repeatedly unsuccessful in reaching her husband, in getting him to value her more. He, like her father, was more responsive to his his parents and his siblings, than to the patient.

The patient's lover, Y., was showing through his conflicted passion that Mrs. Rabin was desired, a person of substance, a gratification for a frustrated, cherished desire.

I felt perplexed and uncomfortable during the session. The patient was putting into me her own conflicted puzzlement. I realized that what I was feeling were the same feelings Mrs. Rabin must have felt, those of bewilderment, anger, and a heightened sense of being controlled by the patient. I interpreted that she enjoyed bewildering and controlling men, myself included, because she had been and was so bewildered by significant men in her own life.

She laughed and said, "I feel sorry for bewildered, tormented men. I want to give to them."

I stored away for future interpretation the hypothesis that Mrs. Rabin wanted to cause men to feel they were nothing because she felt that all the significant men in her life had rendered her superfluous. I was puzzled about her way of getting me to understand, through projective identification, what it was like for her to grow up in a home where women, herself and her mother, were slighted. The grandfather probably was the only exception for the patient.

Upon further reflection, I realized that, through the romantic projective identification inserted into me, I had been induced to participate in a Victorian romantic novel. I visualized the patient's pleased grin and shining eyes as she recounted her lover's tormented, passionate pacing back and forth. I heard inwardly the escalating lyrics, "He loves me. He loves me. Yes, he loves me." I had become her grandfather, who, as I endeavored to interpret and explain to the patient the dynamics behind her compulsive romantic involvement, was in a sense talking poetry to her. No wonder she was excited. Mrs. Rabin was in the paranoid-schizoid position of unreality, of "princes and princesses," and I had countertransferentially joined her in her romantic phantasy. She was also using the manic defense of magical denial to perpetuate a superficial "love" relationship. Understanding better the dynamics of my countertransference, I could hopefully begin interpretations of the patient's self-destructive romantic script.

8

Transference

Almost from the very beginning of Klein's career, she never departed from the fundamental concept of transference, even in her pioneering treatment of children. Klein found derivatives of transference everywhere in the analytic process. She advised that the analyst/therapist safeguard the formation of the transference by avoiding advice, suggestions, or reassurance. For Klein, the basic heartbeat of therapy was anxieties and the defenses against them, whether paranoid-schizoid or depressive, and the therapist needed to interpret the transference resistances depending on the most emergent anxiety. If this procedure was followed, especially with regard to the negative transference, anxiety would be reduced, resistances eroded, splitting diminished, and significant phantasies exposed and worked through.

Whenever the patient feels or imagines that he is made uncomfortable, frustrated, and not understood, he or she will re-experience paranoid-schizoid anxieties and a negative transference. The patient will feel envious, resentful, and persecuted by the therapist. Those adults who as infants had trouble accepting gratification after frustration have greater aggressiveness and more difficulty navigating successfully through the paranoid-schizoid position. They are more likely to manifest a transference colored by the paranoid-schizoid position.

If the adult has had the infantile experience of a bad nourishing breast/mommy in the paranoid-schizoid position, through introjection and projection, he or she establishes alternately an idealized and a persecuting transference.

If the adult as an infant reached the depressive position, a developmental organization characterized by a more integrated ego, the transference will reflect synthesized good and bad projected objects and depressive anxiety—that is, a concern about harming the good breast/mommy (i.e., the therapist). This leads to guilt, anxiety about greed, and a desire to repair any damage to the good breast/mommy (i.e., the therapist).

When the Oedipus complex occurs during the depressive position, the adult carries forward anxiety and guilt from infancy; this leads to a transference that embodies the projective identification of the bad internal objects and the introjection of good external objects. It also leads to splitting, or to the attachment of hate and anxiety to some objects or guilt and reparation to other objects.

If the anxieties associated with the depressive position are not worked through due to manic defenses (e.g., denial, triumph, omnipotence, arrogance), the transference will be shallow and superficial. Insights will also be ephemeral.

WHAT IS THE KEY ELEMENT IN THE KLEINIAN VIEW OF TRANSFERENCE?

The key to the Kleinian understanding of transference resides in the following statement by Melanie Klein (1952b): "I hold that transference originates in the same processes which in the earliest stages determine object-relations. Therefore we have to go back again and again in analysis to the fluctuations between objects, loved and hated, external and internal, which dominate early infancy" (p. 53).

Klein (1952b) emphasized the analysis of the negative transferences as a significant path toward deeper levels of the patient's mind. Aggression, she felt, had been undervalued in therapy.

The therapist may represent a father, a mother, part of the patient's self, the superego, or a number of other internalized objects. No matter what the patient talks about, he will inevitably depict splitting, seeing the therapist as either a good or a bad persecutor or an idealized object. The patient may also express persecutory and depressive anxieties, guilt, envy, greed, reparation, and aspects of his unconscious phantasy life.

Joseph (1985), for example, stresses the analyst's awareness of how patients act on us; how they attempt to pull us into their defensive system; how they capture us so that we may act out. In essence, Joseph emphasizes our countertransference feelings.

Sometimes we may miss the really essential underlying transferences, ignoring the pressures brought to bear on us. We may miss how the patient is seeing or really using us (e.g.

the therapist as the uncomprehending or seductive mother or father, or the patient as the misunderstood or excited infant).

The patient will more likely hear our interpretations in a less distorted fashion the closer he is to the depressive position. Within the paranoid-schizoid position, the patient may hear interpretations as criticisms and/or accusations.

WHAT IS AN EXAMPLE OF A TRANSFERENCE CHARACTERIZED BY AN ATTEMPT TO CONTROL THE THERAPIST?

The patient, Mr. Landis, worried about his excessive criticality. No one escaped his keen observation of his or her defects. His parents, particularly his father, appeared to the patient as weak and vacuous. The patient similarly thought of his girlfriend as dependent and weak. She would easily dissolve into tears whenever Mr. Landis showed any displeasure. While he found her less than adequate, the two times he ended the relationship, he experienced great emptiness, loneliness, and depression.

Although the patient found himself again thinking that he would like to end his relationship with his girlfriend, he hesitated because he did not want to hurt her. He felt this same concern whenever he hurt anyone with his criticality.

In therapy we traced how Mr. Landis was projecting into his parents as well as into his girlfriend the needy, vulnerable parts of his self. He hated that aspect of his self, and when both his parents and his girlfriend were not tuned in to him, he felt persecuted by this bad part of his self that he had put into them.

As I listened to the patient, I felt that I was being pushed into two roles: that of a harsh collaborator with Mr. Landis's sadistic, tormenting criticality of his parents and girlfriend, who desperately wanted to please him, and that of a sympathizer to his disappointment with his insensitive parents and girlfriend. I shared with Mr. Landis how he was forcing me into these two possible roles. This transference interpretation led him to think of his previous therapy. Although he had gone over his ambivalence toward his parents and girlfriend numerous times, he still was not able to free himself from his draining conflictual feelings. I understood his last remark as his way of splitting off the healthy part of his self and placing the understanding self in me, while he took the nonempathic, shallow aspect of his self elsewhere. Mr. Landis was warning me that I could fail, as had the previous therapist, if I thought I was reaching him. When I failed, he would then not have to accept any responsibility for change. I then interpreted that Mr. Landis was setting me up to fail so that he could persecute me with his criticism and persecute himself with guilt. He volunteered that he was able somehow to get people to labor mightily to please him and they, to their chagrin, always failed. Their failure pleased and hurt him at the same time.

WHAT IS AN EXAMPLE OF AN IDEALIZING TRANSFERENCE RESISTANCE?

I noticed that Mrs. Edelman (discussed on page 29 and in Chapter 12) would not add any feeling or idea to an interpretation, but instead behaved as if I had not spoken. She seemed always to be pressed for time, wanting to fill me with

proof of her competence, desirability, and wonderfully generous qualities. Her almost every utterance cried out, "Notice
me! Love me! Pay attention to me!" I did not feel, however,
that she was narcissistic. She showed that she was capable of
appropriate concern and could show suffering, depression,
or guilt. In short, Mrs. Edelman seemed to be closer to the
depressive position.

Mrs. Edelman was perceiving me transferentially as the
idealized object or idealized nourishing breast more in the
paranoid-schizoid position than in the depressive position.
To defend against envy of me, she counted the hours to the
weekly session. More than once she said that she did not
know what she would do without me. All her sense of her
own good qualities, for example, intelligence, love of life,
humor, and caring, were projected into me. By devaluing
herself, she strengthened her defense against envying me. By
contrast, as part of the splitting process, she portrayed her
husband as a "joke," a disgusting, womanly man, a tor-
menter and a chronic critic. I, on the other hand, was "life."
He was "death." I was her combined oedipal mother and
father. If she could introject me, she could repair her mother
and obtain her father's potency.

All the above dynamics had to be interpreted in the
context not only of an idealizing transference resistance but
of an erotic one as well. The patient at first denied that she
had any erotic feelings toward me, believing that I was
merely a necessary mentor who was guiding her toward
ultimate freedom from a horrible marriage. Later she was
able to acknowledge that she did have a phantasy that once
she was free of her husband, she could be married to me. Her
idealization of me began to weaken when she admitted that
she was concerned that I might have some negative qualities
that could impair our possible marriage. With the tentative

admission of some ambivalence, Mrs. Edelman had now entered the depressive position.

> # GIVE AN EXAMPLE OF HOW A PATIENT'S TRANSFERENCE CAN BE REFLECTED IN THE THERAPIST'S BEHAVIOR IN SUPERVISION.

The supervisee hesitatingly admitted that she had held back discussing a particular patient, Mr. Jackson, a young man she had been seeing in psychotherapy for four months on a twice-per-week basis. "You see," she said, "I've had so many other crises with my other patients that Mr. Jackson just didn't seem to need any supervisory input." I wondered privately whether perhaps the supervisee's problem with the patient may very well be his seeming cooperation and the seeming tranquility of treatment (i.e., no resistances, crises, negative transference). I waited for her to continue.

"The patient is a bear of a guy, a policeman. He loves his job. Loves the risk-taking, but I can't seem to get him to elaborate or explore his feelings about his relationship to his wife or anything. Whenever I push, he says, 'Help me out,' or 'I don't know.' " She felt puzzled and thrown off balance by Mr. Jackson's smiling, amiable exterior, which covered up his stubborn passivity and lack of self-reflection. I then asked the supervisee to ponder the paradox of Mr. Jackson, the risk-taking policeman, and Mr. Jackson, the passive, helpless, unknowing patient.

Transferentially, the patient was projecting into the

therapist the active, risk-taking part of his self, the policeman, while at the same time he split off the passive part of his
self, the inert, charmingly dependent patient. I shared this
observation, and the supervisee confirmed that the patient's
wife frequently complained that her husband was removed
and tormented her with his benevolent passivity.

GIVE AN EXAMPLE OF AN ASPECT OF NEGATIVE TRANSFERENCE.

"I am really worried about this patient, Ray Radford," began
the supervisee (Dr. Stephen Block), a well-trained psychologist-
psychoanalyst. I braced myself for some vexing, fulminating
pathology.

Ray is a 17-year-old, "nerdy" high school senior with a
strange appearance, coupled with a flat voice that is wobbly
in pitch. He is the butt of jokes at the school. He does,
however, have one very close friend.

The patient appreciates the value of therapy and has said
on numerous occasions that he considers the therapist his
"lifeline."

When at home, Ray compulsively masturbates and
obsessively kicks the laundry basket. He feels anxious and
guilty concerning his masturbation and other obsessional
rituals.

According to the supervisee, the main source of Ray's
anxiety and tension is his parents. The father has a bad
temper and is very intimidating. As the supervisee put it, "He
even frightens me." The mother is also very critical and
comments on anything that she considers not perfect. For

example, she offered unsolicited criticisms concerning the therapist's office decor. She will not hesitate to offer suggestions to anyone. The supervisee volunteered that sometimes he has the fantasy of strangling both parents.

From a Kleinian perspective, the patient is being persecuted by two angry, frightening, critical parents. He has introjected them, and, functioning within the paranoid-schizoid position, feels that his sexuality and identity as a male is being attacked. His compulsive masturbation is his desperate attempt to shore up his fragmented self. Ray has projected his own murderous rage (e.g., displaced kicking of the laundry basket) into the therapist, who readily verbalizes in his phantasy (e.g., the urge to strangle the parents) his rageful impulses. The patient is trying to carve out a place for himself where he has one measure of control away from the critical disapproval of his parents. Apparently he has reached the depressive position, insofar as he can experience the therapist's concern and express some concern for himself. However, there is a latent negative transference, that is, distrust, that Ray will not as yet share. He will not share details of his masturbatory fantasies.

I suggested to the supervisee that he analyze the distrust and focus on the split between the patient's recognition of the supervisee as his "lifeline" and the simultaneous presence of his distrust of that same idealized object.

9

The Dream

CAN YOU PRESENT A DREAM THAT CAPTURES THE KLEINIAN INNER PHANTASY WORLD?

Beset by a driving ambition to make a lot of money and attain fame, Mr. Lambert, a theoretical physicist, was abandoning his family emotionally without realizing it until his depressed wife brought the fact to his attention with a threat of divorce. Although the patient was pushed into therapy, he seemed to be earnestly working on himself.

Six months of once-per-week therapy have passed and Mr. Lambert brought in the following dream:

> I am walking past Brooklyn State Hospital [a psychiatric facility] and I see a house next to it. I look through an open window and there are two older, Italian-looking women. They are dressed in black. One holds a baby out to me and says, "Take this baby. We cannot keep her any longer. Her teeth are growing through the top of her head." I feel a very painful conflict between wanting to run and wanting to take the baby. I take the baby. I then go home and my wife is upset that I took a damaged baby. The dream ends with me thinking about which agency I could bring the baby to, but I really wanted to keep the baby, to help her.

I asked for associations.

"Brooklyn State is where the 'crazies' were kept in my old neighborhood."

I winced at the term "crazies," but recognized that the patient was using a derisive epithet to deny the anxiety that he was beginning to feel about his own possible "craziness." According to the Kleinian model, the fear of being made crazy by therapy is a powerful initial anxiety, as is the fear of driving the therapist crazy.

Mr. Lambert continued, "The two Italian women looked like widows dressed in black mourning dresses. The baby looked like your typical baby, helpless, pretty, except for the huge teeth growing through the top of her head. That was weird! Makes me think of what I once heard about the saber-toothed tigers. They were supposed to have died out because their two big front teeth kept growing and destroyed their skull cavity.

My wife can't deal with any additional stress now, especially bad stuff coming from me. She's had it."

The patient's dream captures the main elements of his internal phantasy world and what must be addressed in therapy if he is to repair himself and his marriage.

At the paranoid-schizoid position, he becomes terrified of going crazy because of the splitting and projection that dominate his thinking. At some level he may feel guilty (depressive position), though he is displaying denial that he has driven his wife crazy. She is depressed. The two Italian women represent his own confused, contradictory feelings about therapy. On the one hand, he wants to help the "baby," clearly himself, and on the other hand, he wants to run away from therapy by giving up the baby.

Mr. Lambert represents his possible emotional demise with his associations to the saber-toothed tiger. The growth of the teeth, his father's penis that he introjects, can destroy him so that he eventually becomes extinct. In this case, the patient's continued concentration on living cognitively within his head, excluding any attachment to his family, can lead to psychosis, he fears, or to the death of his marriage. Something has to be done to halt these impending catastrophes.

The Italian women and his wife could very well be me. He may wonder if he can give his dependent, damaged, helpless self over to me, and will I be a safe container for him. He is not sure how much he can deal with the damaged-baby aspect of himself on his own. He may also be cautioning me to go easy and to carefully titrate interpretations so as not to make him psychotic. His own statements suggest caution, for example, "My wife can't deal with any additional stress now, especially bad stuff coming from me. She's had it." Above all else, he is anxious about the possibility that he can be repaired or dreads that he will destroy the therapist with his psychotic anxieties.

WHAT IS ANOTHER EXAMPLE OF A PATIENT'S DREAM AND HOW WOULD IT BE UNDERSTOOD FROM A KLEINIAN PERSPECTIVE?

The patient, Mrs. Fabian, a 40-year-old divorcée and an accountant, began the session with a dream introduced as follows: "I had a funny dream last night." Knowing the patient by now rather well (she had been in once-per-week therapy for two years), I suspected that her use of the word "funny" meant "painful and depressing." I waited for confirmation of my initial hunch.

Her dream is as follows:

> I attended a rally or dinner and the President of the United States was there. I shook his hand and said, "I disagree with Hillary Clinton about two different issues." He said, "Thank you." I walked away thinking, "Hillary is not just any old political person, but his wife. How could I have said that to him?!"

Her associations were as follows. To "Hillary," she said that a political rally was something she would never attend in real life. Therefore it was highly unlikely that she would ever meet Hillary there. She was not really involved in politics of any sort. She was only able to express herself assertively through written communication. As she put it, "I'm such a rabbit in a group or social situation." Speaking up implied to Mrs. Fabian scary risk-taking and self-confidence. She avoided this, "because then you would have to deal with a person's reaction to your remarks."

To "President Clinton," the patient associated a similarity to President Kennedy. "There is something about him. Maybe he will make it better than Bush." She recalled that there had been political discussions at the dinner table the evening prior to the dream.

To "Hillary Clinton," Mrs. Fabian also connected the Jewish custom of saying prayers for a departed loved parent. Hillary Clinton's father had just died at the time that the patient had finished saying prayers for her deceased father.

The patient then went on to say that her entire past week had been a "disaster," very distressing. She had invited her new daughter-in-law and her son, and another older son's family to dinner. Unfortunately everyone except her new daughter-in-law had become ill shortly after dinner because of food poisoning. Her new daughter-in-law had escaped this trauma because she had insisted on eating her own religiously prescribed kosher food. Mrs. Fabian disliked her for her pushiness and arrogant narcissism. "Just before dinner, for example, she announced loudly that she had read somewhere how a family and their guests had all gotten food poisoning at a family gathering." The patient, of course, realized that there was no reality to her subsequent paranoid idea that her new daughter-in-law had indeed poisoned the family, but it almost seemed as if she did.

In addition, the patient's 80-year-old mother was particularly harmed by the food poisoning and, to add insult to injury, the grandmother had to sleep on an uncomfortable couch, since the new daughter-in-law refused to sleep on anything other than a comfortable, spacious bed.

The patient had also shared with her younger son at dinner that other members of the family were angry with him for not helping out enough with the food preparation and clean-up. He had become defensive and his wife, the new daughter-in-law, had rushed to his defense like a lioness protecting her threatened young. The patient, of course, deeply regretted the food poisoning, but also felt guilty and foolish telling her son of his family's displeasure concerning his lack of participation, that he had not done his fair share. She also felt animosity toward her new daughter-in-law, who, she believed, had considerably added to the emotional turmoil of that evening.

With all the above in mind, what can we make of the patient's dream and her rich associations from a Kleinian perspective?

The patient prefaced her dream as "funny." As I'd suspected, the dream and the subsequent associations to it revealed a particularly depressing, humiliating recent episode. Both the paranoid-schizoid and the depressive positions appear to be present, that is, in the food-poisoning belief concerning her new daughter-in-law, in the patient's guilt over her tactless remarks to her son and, in the dream, to President Clinton, and, of course, in her guilt concerning the food poisoning.

There were many splits occurring, originating from both positions. The patient, within the paranoid-schizoid position, felt persecuted by President Clinton's wife, who represented her new daughter-in-law and her son. She also split along the following lines: (1) the idealized, social, expansive, assertive self, versus the timid "rabbit," self; (2) the self that poisoned everyone through spoiling the good, versus the self that could repair and protect a husband like Hillary Clinton in her dream, versus the self who failed to improve and defend her own former husband (Mrs. Fabian had not succeeded in alleviating her ex-husband's considerable schizoid pathology); and (3) A self that could withstand considerable adversity and confidently take care of itself, for example, Hillary Clinton and her daughter-in-law's escape from food poisoning, versus a self that broke down into timidity and avoidance of open confrontation. The patient was envious of

Hillary Clinton's status conferred by her powerful husband and her daughter-in-law's status conferred through marriage to the patient's son. She envied Hillary Clinton's confident assertiveness and as well as her daughter-in-law's confident yet tactless assertion of her needs. She also felt devalued by both of them. They were married to powerful, capable men (i.e., she sometimes saw her younger son as very capable and potent). She, however, had no significant man in her life, and her former husband, at first looking very capable, had turned out to be timid, weak, and passive. For decades he had figuratively and literally hidden from life by working for long hours in the basement of their home.

The patient's paranoid-like speculation about her daughter-in-law's possible poisoning of them, although she quickly discounted it, was the product of Mrs. Fabian's animosity toward her daughter-in-law, a projective identificatory wish to get rid of her and the phantasied retaliation of her daughter-in-law in answer to the wish. The patient also envied both Hillary Clinton's and her daughter-in-law's relationship with the strong, capable men from whom they partly derived their confident assertiveness.

Within the depressive position, the patient displayed great guilt and concern over the food poisoning and over her tactless comments to both President Clinton in her dream and her younger son during the dinner. She had also failed to protect her family and former husband, she believed, from her own spoiling, destructive impulses. Her sense of reality, however, was still intact. She was aware that her passing thought that her daughter-in-law had poisoned them was foolish and not at all possible. She also accepted, without question, responsibility for the accidental poisoning.

The patient's father had been an unsuccessful businessman and she perceived him as a likable and passive man who was readily manipulated by her mother's tactless assertiveness. She tended to project her passive self into others, particularly her newly married younger son. She also tended to project into others her mother's confident insensitivity, particularly into women, for example, her younger son's wife. She disliked the paranoid and insensitive aspects of her self, but was less aware of the idealized, powerful, spoiling part of her self.

At the beginning of therapy, Mrs. Fabian perceived me transferentially as the understanding father and her ally against persecuting family members and work associates. She also saw me as a container able to take in her projective identifications and not fragment into self-pity or depression. I, in turn, experienced her self-pity and sense of being beleaguered by a good part of the world, for example, her family or colleagues. I felt that she experienced me as particularly close to her when she evacuated into me her pain, humiliation, envy, and guilt. I inferred that the patient's greatest anxiety concerned her spoiling propensities through passivity and insensitive criticality. Interpretations were directed toward this aspect of her self and her envy of confident women who had had the good fortune to introject strong, respected fathers.

IN A PATIENT'S INTERNAL WORLD, ONE ASPECT OF THAT WORLD CAN BE IN CONFLICT WITH ANOTHER. CAN YOU PRESENT MATERIAL THAT CLEARLY ILLUSTRATES THIS INNER BATTLE?

Mrs. Karp, a 45-year-old divorced woman, had begun therapy on a once-per-week basis, two years ago. Too self-effacing and unable to stand up for her needs and wishes, she had allowed an ex-husband, lover, and son to manipulate and exploit her.

The patient had made some progress. She could now exercise a greater degree of appropriate self-concern and take responsibility for her passivity. In other words, Mrs. Karp was more in the depressive position, but she still needed to consolidate her gains; she needed to exercise a more reliable control over her splitting, which fostered a tendency to act self-destructively. She would give in to her passive self and ignore her autonomous, self-preservative, healthy self.

During the session to be discussed, she reported two dreams as follows.

In the first dream the patient was back at college with her college friends. The room was beautiful. Everybody was dressed nicely. Mrs. Karp was talking to someone whom she could not identify. She then realized that she had forgotten her coat, but she was not apologetic about not having the coat.

I asked for the day residue. On the day preceding the dream, the patient recalled, she had had an image of a desert mesa upon which rested the skeletal remains of a cow's rib cage. It had no guts. The patient spontaneously added that her dream, unlike the skeletal rib cage of the cow, had guts. In her dream she had shown guts. Her ex-husband used to derisively refer to her as a "cow," a woman who was empty and placidly agreeable to being controlled by him or anyone else.

Her associations led to happy memories of college and her assertion that not having the coat felt right to her.

I said, "You are more comfortable with who you are now."

This interpretation led the patient to describe a recent shopping outing with C., a close female friend and colleague. C. is considerably wealthier than Mrs. Karp.

"I went shopping with C.," she said. "I was very conscious of how much C. could buy as against the little I could buy. But I saw that C. was also hurting and I was concerned for her. Thank God I am not where she is!

First expressing envy from the paranoid-schizoid position, the patient was able to validate her growth through increased self-acceptance. She could then get in touch with her capacity to be concerned with C. more from the depressive position.

Her second dream is as follows:

> I am in the kitchen. Sitting at one end of an oval table is my father, reading a newspaper, and at the other end of the table is my brother. I am standing there with my apron on. I wonder where my mother is. I ask my father and he says in a harsh voice, without looking up from his paper, "Don't you remember? I told you!" I stamp my foot and say angrily back, "No, I don't remember what you told me!" Just at that moment, a little spotted dog comes running from upstairs into the room. I remember thinking, That's a funny-looking dog.

The patient's associations went back to her childhood and to memories of her father and her mother. She painfully recalled how her father did not speak to her much. She always wanted to stay away from him because he treated her harshly. There were so many "shoulds." Her mother, too, was oblivious to her. Father ran away to work. Her exhusband was the same way as her father. He would say to her with great contempt and disdain in his voice, "All right, I'll explain it to you again," as if the patient was a retarded child.

The dog reminded the patient of her former boyfriend, F. She had at first felt sorry for him. He had a dog that was always yapping. The dog was very irritating. F. called him "Octane" because he had found him in a gas station, chained pathetically to a post. The patient's brother also had a dog that would kill rats in her father's factory.

Once again Mrs. Karp has demonstrated an increasing capacity to stand up for herself. Now, she does not allow her father to contemptuously dismiss her. Formerly, her father and her brother apparently did not serve as a replacement container for her absent mother. I said to Mrs. Karp that at times she had dismissed herself as her father had done to her in the dream and as her ex-husband, former lover, and older brother had similarly behaved. The patient associated "gas" to "Octane," the dog's name, which is used to fuel a car. She was able to see that she was both a poor, abused dog yearning to be cared for, and "octane" looking to fuel the replacements for her father and brother.

Both dreams demonstrated that Mrs. Karp was becoming more irritated with that part of her split self that viewed itself as desperately empty and idealizing of nongratifying adults. At the same time, she was beginning to challenge her past projections of her own neediness into her ex-husband and former boyfriend. She was finding that she had substance, "guts," and was no longer the desperate, abused little child begging to be filled up or needing to feed greedy others. I say greedy others because her father, brother, and ex-husband had all been abusive alcoholics.

Transferentially, I am the older brother in the dream, admired and idealized. The patient is very careful not to express hostility except in the mildest manner. The interpretation and working through of the negative transference is particularly difficult with Mrs. Karp, because she insists on preserving me in an idealized form, that is, as a "nice, understanding, kind man." The role of therapist, of course, encourages patients to perceive the therapist as nice and kindly, since the therapist in truth strives to be nonjudgmental and understanding. This is another barrier to the encouragement of the patient's expression of anger.

> # GIVE AN EXAMPLE OF A DREAM THAT EXPRESSES CONCERN FOR ANOTHER PERSON, A VITAL ACCOMPLISHMENT OF THE DEPRESSIVE POSITION.

Mrs. Garber, a 45-year-old professional, had finally ended her marriage, one that had been empty and terribly painful for many years. She had lately complained of being confused, depressed, and cut off from family and friends. Following is her most recent dream.

> Leila Kelly was pregnant. I said something about her little sister having a daughter, and I said to her that she too could have a daughter.
>
> In the next scene, I was explaining to Dr. Solomon how the name Alexander could be used as a Hebrew or Jewish name.
>
> Next scene: There was a disagreement with my son, Michael. I wanted to reach him. His wife, Betty, put on a blond "Annie" wig. She told him to go home. I said to her that we are not fighting. That's how we are. She could not accept that we were merely having an intellectual discussion.
>
> Next scene: I heard that Israel had made a law of return (i.e., any Jew can become a citizen of Israel) only for families. It was being challenged and then I heard a voice saying in Yiddish, "*Einer est ich a mensch*" (One person is also a person worthy of respect).

The day of the dream the patient had had a CAT scan to discover a possibly dangerous ear growth. She had been feeling that she was falling apart.

Her associations to Leila Kelly in her dream were that

Leila was really pregnant. Leila was very little, tiny, very attractive, and intellectual. Her husband, Jack, was also very bright. He was going to be a lawyer, was already a political activist, and was an assistant to Rabbi Allen (the same name as the patient's older son). The patient's associations led to her realization that she was feeling more and more disconnected from her younger son, thanks to her new daughter-in-law. She was also envious of younger women's capacity to become pregnant and, at the same time, she was depressed that she was alone, without any husband. Her daughter had recently informed her that she would not name any child she had in accordance with the patient's wishes. This thought came from her dream segment as an explanation for the name Alexander. The patient also envied Leila Kelly's sister-in-law, Mrs. V. The patient would have liked to have a daughter-in-law such as Mrs. V. apparently had. The patient was becoming more and more disenchanted with her daughter-in-law.

The dream finally ends on a reassuring note capturing a main element, concern, central to the depressive position. The patient hears a voice coming from the internal soothing maternal and/or paternal object (she could not identify whether the voice was male or female), which reminded her of her intactness and worth. If the patient can listen and take this voice to heart, she will be less fragmented and split. She will feel her worth as an individual without the need for continual relatedness to every member of her family. In addition, her daughter-in-law and her daughter, seen from the paranoid-schizoid position now as persecutors, can later be viewed from the depressive position in less black-and-white terms.

CAN YOU PRESENT A DREAM GIVEN DURING THE TERMINATING PHASE?

Many years of once-per-week sessions had passed since Mr. Olsen began therapy. Now 50 years of age and happily married, he was no longer an alcoholic, a womanizer, and an explosive participant in barroom brawls. The following is a dream he brought in during the termination phase of therapy.

> The patient went into a medical office to see a doctor for an examination. The doctor appeared familiar but shadowy. In the next room there was a Dr. Goodman. Mr. Olsen told the shadowy doctor that he did not understand why Dr. Goodman was there to examine him considering that he had been unhappy with Dr. Goodman and no longer used him as his physician. Nonetheless, Dr. Goodman examined him, with the insertion of a needle through his wrist. The needle was quite long and blood began to spurt.

The patient explained that the day of the dream he had been out gardening. It was a really nice day. He had helped his wife and two other women who lived next door with their garden. He then associated his father to the shadowy doctor. He felt warm in the presence of the doctor and trusted him. It was almost as if the doctor reminded him of his father, although he very rarely remembered having any warm feelings toward his despotic father. The rare good times with his father were during gardening. His father enjoyed planting and would encourage the patient when he was very young to help him in the garden. These were warm, close moments.

"Goodman" in his dream was not really good. He did

not listen, did not belong there, and inflicted pain. I interpreted that what Mr. Olsen had once thought of as "good": self-destructive acting out that included fighting, exploitation of women, and alcoholism, he no longer regarded as "good." He added that he no longer saw his father in black-and-white terms, that is, ogre versus omnipotent protector. The patient had moved from the paranoid-schizoid position of splitting to the depressive position, wherein he saw his father more ambivalently. He could also make a commitment to a woman, enjoy giving, be creative, and be concerned with another human being.

CAN YOU PRESENT A DREAM THAT ILLUSTRATES THE MANIC DEFENSE OF MAGICAL REPARATION?

The patient, Mrs. Sable, 41 years of age, had a terrible marriage. She tried to keep away from her husband as much as possible, and to some extent she succeeded. However, weekends were the most difficult times for her, for despite her husband's verbal abuse, he still expected her to be sexually available to him. Sometimes the patient gave in just to placate her husband and perhaps to manipulate him to meet a need she might have. She realized that she was manipulating her husband, but felt that married life would be unbearable if she did not from time to time comply with his sexual demands. In short, Mrs. Sable felt trapped between wanting to leave her husband and end her marriage, and the anxiety of being economically on her own.

During the week the patient experienced the following dream:

It was a horrible nightmare. My husband was trying to break
into the apartment. The door was slightly open. I tried to call
the police but no one answered. I met Fred, a lover, outside
and said, "Maybe we should take a cab to Greenwich
Village." He wanted to know what happened, but I said, "I
can't tell you." Then I decided to go to my brother Billy's
house. I thought, "Thank God it's only a dream," and he said,
"You must be guilty about something."

The patient told her dream to her husband and he
became furious. He shouted at her that she was guilty over
something. Mrs. Sable did indeed feel guilty. She had had an
affair a number of years ago that was discovered by her
husband, and he would bring the affair up every time he was
angry with her.

I suspected that the patient had shared her dream with
her husband to communicate how much she felt threatened
and attacked by him. He predictably got the message, but
also predictably attacked her for daring to tell him that he
mistrusted her.

The patient associated to her husband as someone trying
to find out what was going on in her life and to her wish to
keep him out. Her associations to the door being slightly
open were her attempts to keep the marriage going through
sex. What scared her most about her husband was the way he
believed he could abuse her one minute, then act aggrieved
when she refused to treat him with affection. The police in
the dream were supposed to rescue her but they failed.

Mrs. Sable was not sure about Fred. He is a man at her
job who seems somewhat effeminate. Her brother, Billy,
meant possible safety, but not complete safety. She also felt
that she has disappointed her family by not ending her
marriage a long time ago.

Listening to the patient's dream, I felt sad that she still
did not seem to get the message. She kept thinking that she

could make what seemed an intolerable marital situation tolerable, or believed that she could reach her husband so that he would change. She was not accepting her own need to change. Neither the police in her dream, namely me, nor the effeminate man, namely her former lover, nor her brother could rescue her. Mrs. Sable was in the grip of a manic defense of magical reparation. She had to choose to fully close the door on her husband. A part of her obviously wanted to end her marriage, but another aspect of her self wanted to remain passive and be rescued by me. I began my interpretation by asking her about her phantasy of being rescued by a man. My understanding, of course, had to become hers in time.

10

Termination

Melanie Klein (1950) wrote a short paper "On the Criteria for the Termination of a Psychoanalysis," which contained her main ideas and the goals hopefully reached toward the end of treatment.

She states that there are two kinds of anxieties: paranoid-schizoid and depressive. The therapist ought to see a working through of the depressive anxiety, therefore perceiving the patient as better able to see life more realistically, to preserve love better, to repair relationships, and to experience reason able, appropriate guilt. The patient ought to have established good internalized helpful, protective objects, and gotten in touch with some degree of love toward his or her parent or parents. The patient ought to feel that he or she can satisfy a partner sexually and be more considerate and appropriately concerned with others. The patient should have an increased phantasy life and a richer, variegated emotional life as well.

As regards working through of the paranoid-schizoid position toward the end of therapy, the patient ought to be free of hypochondriacal anxiety and free of fears of being attacked and devalued. There ought to be less idealization of the therapist and, in particular, less idealization of others in general. This means that the negative as well as the positive transference must be worked through to get to the rest of the depressive and paranoid-schizoid anxieties. Splitting must be reduced between the idealized internal objects and persecutory objects. As Klein (1950) states, "Good objects — as distinct from idealized ones — can be securely established in the mind only if the strong split between persecutory and ideal figures has diminished, if aggressive and libidinal impulses have come closer together and hatred has become mitigated by love" (p. 47).

Finally, the patient ought not to be manifesting manic defenses, which result in a superficial facade of togetherness but a shallow emotional life.

WHAT IS AN EXAMPLE OF THE AVOIDANCE OF A PRECIPITOUS TERMINATION?

The patient, Mrs. Eaton, had been in therapy for a year and six months. She entered therapy complaining of a bad marriage. She was finding herself perpetually angry with her husband. He was not living up to her expectations. She resented that she always had to make decisions and assume responsibility. She also had other problems. Her main obsessions were fantasies about various priests. When asked for details about the obsessions, she would not reveal anything specific. It was almost as if, by exposing details of her obsessions, some degree of pleasure would be taken away from her. Mrs. Eaton denied that her obsessions were in any way sexual. However, she did behave in a flirtatious way with the therapist.

Her family background is as follows. Her father would not allow the patient as a child to deviate in any way from what he considered proper religious tenets. Her mother was rigid, critical, and guilt-producing. Both parents would not listen to the patient.

During therapy she described how she was excessively critical of her husband. She would first annihilate him by zeroing in on some of his limitations, then feel very guilty and apologize. She would try to make up to her husband for her attacks, but then felt, through her excessive guilt, that her husband would take advantage of her. She was also concerned with what her poor marriage was doing to her 11-year-old boy, who was manifesting behavioral problems in school. Feeling guilt-ridden, the patient went to a priest, who behaved in a cold, rejecting manner. She felt particularly "destroyed" by the priest because she had previously had some romantic obsessions about him. The priest had only talked about the patient's need for absolution, increasing the patient's guilty torment.

Mrs. Eaton then approached another priest toward whom she also had strong romantic feelings. He was not physically attractive but he was aggressively assertive. She experienced him as being too harshly confrontational. He told her, among other things, that her husband was taking unfair advantage of her. (This was an aspect of her marriage that she had not revealed even to her therapist.) The priest cut through her psyche, she claimed, like a knife. She was furious with him at first, then went to him for further counseling. She felt hurt and rejected when he attempted to refer her to another therapist.

Her current therapist, Dr. Stephen Block, while helpful, is diminished in the patient's eyes because he is not like a priest, that is, closer to God. She admitted that she does not trust the therapist. When he brought her flirting with him to her attention, Mrs. Eaton blushed and agreed that she could be flirtatious. According to the therapist, the patient exudes an air of childlike innocence, yet she also is a game player. Even as she communicated a passionate desire to have a closer relationship with the therapist, she announced that she could not continue in therapy. She offered the feeble excuse of a class that she had to take that conflicted with the therapy hour.

In the supervisory session, Dr. Block wanted to know how to avert Mrs. Eaton's anticipated termination of therapy. I suggested that he seemed to back off in his interpretations of the patient's ego splits, which were, from my perspective, as follows: perceiving priests as good, idealized objects, and her husband as the bad object, seeing the therapist as not to be trusted, versus complete trust in priests; desiring to flirt and seduce, versus prudish, angelic innocence; and a part of her self that moves toward the therapist, versus an aspect of her self that wants to terminate.

I asked the supervisee to consider the possibility that he was countertransferring by validating, through his timidity, Mrs. Eaton's projective identification into him of an asexual "priest" who could not be trusted, and a husband she viewed with contempt. I shared my hunch that the patient had introjected her critical, arrogant, detached parents and was excessively projecting them into her husband and her therapist. Her anger was merely muffled, and emerged as distrust and a kind of sexual teasing. It seemed to me that the patient was projecting into the therapist her defense against the sadistic aspect of herself, and the therapist had introjected this part of the patient. The therapist had become immobilized and impotent through this introjection. Apparently when one priest brutally assaulted the patient with "insights," the patient, though at first furious, returned for further counseling. Could it be that she was trying to provoke a sadistic attack? If so, perhaps a more forceful, but not sadistic, confrontation dealing with the patient's teasing might halt her desire to terminate and put therapy back on track.

GIVE AN EXAMPLE OF THE CONSEQUENCES OF ACTING OUT ON TERMINATION.

The supervisee who treated the twin, Ms. Tash (see page 105), was correct when she reacted initially to the patient with a sense of foreboding. The patient came in for her second session and announced with a satisfied smile that she had had her 15-year-old son placed in a foster home because he was "evil." In a previous supervisory session, we had concluded that the patient would prove extremely difficult to treat because she appeared to be functioning primarily within the paranoid-schizoid position. Then, too, there was the additional complication of her being locked into a dependent symbiotic relationship with her twin sister. In addition, the patient had multiple sclerosis. The first interview had revealed that the patient was filled with envy toward her sister, who did not have the patient's illness.

I asked the supervisee what she felt about the patient's triumphant announcement that she had disposed of her "evil" son.

She replied, "It brought up rage in me. She looked thrilled and relieved. She showed no awareness that she had anything to do with her son's problems.

"The patient then hit me with another 'bomb.' "

I listened.

"She stated that she wanted another therapist. I was too young."

The supervisee was 27 and the patient was 37.

"The patient said that if she were to stay with me as her therapist, she would just be quiet. She felt uncomfortable and unsafe with me.

"I tried to explore why she was so adamant about wanting an older therapist, but she would not budge. Reassurance wouldn't work. It was like hitting a brick wall."

I suggested that the patient had split off the "evil" part of herself and was projecting it into both her son and the supervisee. Her rage was also being projected into the supervisee, explaining why she felt so angry with the patient. With the "evil" part of herself firmly deposited into the therapist and her son, the patient magically believed that she was safe and comfortable. Since the patient was so firmly entrenched in the paranoid-schizoid position, she had no ambivalence and no self-awareness. The only thing the patient feared at this point was that the therapist or her son would put the "evil" back into her that she had put into them. The patient's desire for an older therapist represented a wish for an idealized mother or sister who would merge with the patient and make her omnipotent.

The supervisee, failing to reach the patient, assented to her request for another therapist. I sensed the supervisee's guilt at not connecting with the patient. I reassured her that the patient's projective identifications into the supervisee were predominantly evacuative rather than communicative. To the patient, the supervisee was only a part-object, a devalued breast who could be easily discarded.

The supervisee finished her description of the session.

"As soon as I told her that she could have an older therapist, she said, 'Could I go now?' "

This patient's rigid, immutable resistance illustrates the destructive power of the manic defense of denial, control, and triumph. There is very little healthy ego the supervisee can tap into. Self-awareness, reflection, concern, and guilt are only in the therapist and not in the patient. The patient's excessive projective identifications, envy, and rage have blunted her capacity to introject the supervisee's concern and any offered good. The next "older" therapist may also become the devalued, "evil," persecuting breast to be ultimately destroyed through precipitous termination.

WHAT IS AN INSTANCE OF A THREAT OF TERMINATION THAT WAS DEALT WITH SO THAT THERAPY CONTINUED?

Mr. Quince smiled and began with, "One of us wants to end therapy. Guess which one."

The Quinces had been in marital therapy for a year and a half and had made great progress. They were more affectionate toward each other and considerably less angry with each other. Those arguments or disagreements that they did have were settled quickly and reasonably. I had not decided in my own mind that they were ready for termination, so I was taken by surprise. Mr. and Mrs. Quince had not given any indication that they were interested in ending treatment.

I said, "I guess it's the wife."

He said, "Bingo!"

When I asked why, the wife giggled and turned toward her husband as if she had felt betrayed and guilty and was not yet up to telling me that she no longer wished to continue the sessions.

She said, "Well, things are going well, We can talk and we seem able to settle our differences better."

Mr. Quince interrupted, "I don't want to end. There are things we haven't worked out. Yes, we've made progress, but my wife hasn't worked out her relationship with her mother, and that interferes with our marriage."

"How so?" I asked.

"She won't openly confront her mother when she criticizes or hurts her. Instead, she indirectly comes back at her mother in front of the children. That's not good for them."

Out of the corner of my eye I saw Mrs. Quince's face flush. Her voice rose, "I don't want to confront her. It wouldn't do any good. Besides, our children aren't affected."

We then went back and forth about the effects on the children. Mrs. Quince started to cry. "What do you two want from me? I can't do it. If I yell at her, she will know she got to me. She makes me crazy."

I said softly, "Mrs. Quince, you don't have to do anything now with regard to your mother. Let's just talk about it. Only when you're ready need you say something to her."

Mrs. Quince, relieved of the belief that her husband and I were asking her to attack her mother immediately, then described her past relationship with her mother. Evidently, her mother felt entitled to be critical of everything Mrs. Quince did. By contrast her mother treated her older brother with veneration and pride. Mrs. Quince indicated that, unlike her brother, she had sexually acted out in high school, whereas her brother had led a monastic academic life, and, in fact, was socially inept. What bothered the patient the most was that her mother on occasion still brought up in front of the children or others that Mrs. Quince had been a "bimbo," a "floozy," during her adolescent years. This enraged her, but she did not say anything directly to her mother.

There was no doubt that Mrs. Quince was filled with tremendous rage, so much rage that she feared that she could drive either her mother or herself crazy. Mrs. Quince's mother appeared to be a chronic persecutor of the patient and a difficult woman in general. Certainly Mrs. Quince needed to separate from her mother through appropriate sharing of her hurt when her mother attacked her. According to the husband, the patient sometimes lost control and reacted too much with intense anger and criticism, not only toward him but toward the children as well. She had obviously introjected her mother and was projecting her into others. She was also projecting into her family her own anxiety and frustration built up during her childhood years and still continuing at the hands of her mother. Less obvious is Mrs. Quince's envy of her brother, who appears to have been idealized by the mother.

Mrs. Quince's ego splitting needed to be interpreted so that she could eventually stand up to her mother as a confident adult. These splits were as follows: a self that prized silence as strength in the face of being attacked by her mother, versus confronting her mother and possibly "going crazy"; and a self that was quite capable of standing up for itself with others, versus a self that folded in the face of her mother's capricious attacks.

Mrs. Quince's wish to end therapy was unconsciously a manic attempt to run away from understanding and working through her ongoing grievances against her mother. I told her this in so many words and she agreed that she and her husband needed to continue marital therapy.

WHAT WOULD PROMPT CONSIDERATION OF TERMINATION IN THE NEAR FUTURE?

Mrs. Tanner was looking forward to starting a new life after divorcing her husband. When he had given her an intolerable ultimatum, all the pent-up feelings stemming from his past narcissistic abuses of her burst forth and she ended the marriage. She was young, intelligent, and attractive. She had a good job and was able to move back into the city to resume a single life.

In the session, Mrs. Tanner recounted her latest experience in a singles bar.

"I was sitting there with my girlfriend when Jason came over and sat down next to me. Jason was a guy that I just adored in college. He asked me about my divorce, and then he asked a very upsetting personal question."

"What was that?"

"He wanted to know if I had spotted anything in my ex-husband early in our relationship that should have warned me not to marry him. Just as I started to answer, he turned his back on me and hailed another girl. I just sat there stunned. I felt a rush of anger, then the thought that he's going to feel guilty later on for treating me this way."

"Guilty?"

"No, not really guilty. That's the old me talking. Actually, I heard your voice saying, 'This guy is like your ex-husband—self-centered and inconsiderate.' I remembered an incident with my husband very early in the marriage. We had gone skiing. He was a good skier and I was a novice. We were going up in the lift when I dropped one of my poles. I asked him if I could borrow one of his. He said, 'No!' I had dropped mine and he was not responsible for my accident. He said that I would have to ski down with one pole. I did and I was terrified."

I asked, "What did you feel later?"

"I thought that was a rotten thing to do and some day he'll feel guilty."

"Did he?"

"No."

Before the patient began therapy she was much more within the paranoid-schizoid position. She had not been fully aware of her resentments toward her husband for his callous indifference to her needs. She had projected into him guilt and concern, which he did not feel. Mrs. Tanner had not shown enough concern for herself nor had she felt secure enough to discover her husband's significant lack of concern toward her. She had split him into an individual who would be appropriately guilty in the future versus a person who was self-centered and immature. Using the manic defense of denial, somehow Mrs. Tanner thought she could magically repair her husband so that he would be reflective, aware, and concerned—that is, properly guilty.

Therapy had advanced the patient solidly to the depressive position. When Jason treated her as a part-object, turning his back on her, she could now, using her increased concern for her self and lessened manic denial, see him for what he was, another version of her ex-husband. Hearing the therapist's voice within, she gives evidence that she has introjected the therapist as a helpful internal object, and, from now on, will persecute herself less because of reduced splitting. Consequently, she will not feel driven to select and repair men who cannot be repaired.

11

Narcissism, Masochism, Suicide, and Other Clinical Issues

WHAT IS THE BASIS OF DESTRUCTIVE NARCISSISM?

The arrogant, destructively self-absorbed, narcissistic patient idealizes his self. He maintains the self-idealization through introjects and projective identifications with ideal objects.

The Kleinian therapist has to be very careful not to threaten the vulnerable self-esteem of the narcissistic patient. If it is threatened, the narcissist will experience humiliation and will display sarcasm, scorn, contempt, and rage.

Envy also plays a significant role in the dynamics of

narcissism. As the therapist slowly exposes the patient's self-idealizations, which are based on introjected and projected identifications with idealized objects, destructive envy of the therapist increases. The narcissistic patient desperately wants to believe that he has the idealized internalized breast and does not need to depend on anyone or to obtain help from anyone. Rosenfeld (1987) cautions that narcissistic patients may act out destructively (e.g., be suicidal or have impairment of employment or marriage).

CAN YOU GIVE AN EXAMPLE OF EXTREME NARCISSISTIC BEHAVIOR?

Mr. Davis was used to getting his own way. In school he was a wunderkind and a fine athlete. Gifted with a tenacious memory and a keen analytical mind, he entered the profession of law. There, he did well and, although married, he preyed upon a succession of paralegals employed by his firm. Each time his wife would discover the affair, and each time Mr. Davis would swear that it would not happen again.

Mr. Davis was a very vexing patient. He behaved in an arrogant and adversarial manner. "I disagree" was his most frequent automatic response to any interpretation, no matter how mild. His idealization of himself as the generous, compassionate man was not to be breached. If his wife was hurt, that really was her problem, since his girlfriends were merely friends and the affairs had ended. Mr. Davis used intellect to cancel out feeling. As I struggled to reach Mr. Davis I realized that I was being placed in the same position as his wife. Mr. Davis did not want to depend on anyone, and if he let in my interpretations, he feared that they would increase his dependency on me. This was a consequence that would be too humiliating. He left therapy precipitously and entered treatment with a therapist who emphasized cognition. I subsequently learned that his marriage had ended.

> # THERE ARE CERTAIN INDIVIDUALS WHO EXHIBIT VAMPIRE-LIKE BEHAVIOR. WHAT EXACTLY DOES THIS MEAN?

While Mrs. Tarlow, a professional, worked diligently at a demanding job, her husband spent his time in the basement of their home earning little through a mail-order business. In addition, Mr. Tarlow concealed his gambling from his wife, ultimately placing his family in extreme economic jeopardy. He appeared indifferent to emotional and physical intimacy, and had maintained this attitude for many marital years. To the outside world, Mr. Tarlow was an amiable, charming man who seemed to love socializing, but in the home he retreated into physical and emotional isolation.

As therapy unfolded, the patient described the rather bizarre family background of her husband. Apparently Mr. Tarlow had a brother who had established a successful law practice and then absconded with his clients' money. He also was a pederast. At the present time the brother had fled to a foreign country to avoid extradition. Mr. Tarlow had some similar character traits. He was secretive, detached, and self-destructive. He would justify avoiding the patient on the grounds that she would "drain" him of his energy. The reverse was actually true. Both Mr. Tarlow and his brother had drained their family of origin of every penny. Mr. Tarlow and his brother would even compete with each other as to who could drain the other of his money in a more elegant manner! There are your "vampires."

WHAT IS THE KLEINIAN UNDERSTANDING OF THE PSYCHOPATH'S PERSONALITY?

The psychopathic personality is characterized by a lack of conscious guilt, a sense of specialness, greed, narcissism, and impulsivity. He exploits unhesitatingly and manipulates family members, friends, and strangers.

According to Joseph (1960), the psychopathic personality has a powerful phantasy of being omnipotent based on splitting, and uses projective identification and introjective identification enormously. He idealizes powerful figures and, through introjection, feels a sense of power, avoiding envy and depression. The psychopath splits off his despised self and projects it into surrounding external objects. Massive use of projective identification, however, leads to a sense of emptiness and an intensification of persecutory anxiety.

CAN YOU DESCRIBE A PARTICULAR TYPE OF MASOCHISM?

There is a kind of masochism manifested by certain patients first described by Joseph (1982). These patients show a sense of hopelessness and other self-destructive actions, for example, overwork and poor sleep and eating habits.

Joseph (1982) views these patients as addicted to what she sees as a near-death state. They seem to derive anticipatory pleasure in destroying themselves. Transferentially, these patients attempt to involve the therapist in a collusion with their hopelessness by projecting their despair into the therapist. They want the therapist to attack or criticize them.

What are the dynamics behind the compulsive addiction to near-death? Apparently, the patients feel captured by a part of the self that, like a concentration camp commandant, sadistically torments and imprisons them. Through self-destruction, they gratify in an exciting way the sadistic, imprisoning self. There results a cycle in which the "commandant" torments the vulnerable part of the patient's self, which in turn suffers; this elicits more torment from the sadistic part of the self. In therapy, the patient unconsciously attempts to provoke the therapist to attack him as a representative of his internal sadistic self. The patient is passive and persistently despairing. The therapist needs to become aware of a particular central transference resistance. In spite of the patient's seeming expression of significant material in the sessions, "the analyst seems to be the only person in the room who is actively concerned about change, about progress, about development; as if all the active parts of the patient have been projected into the analyst" (Joseph 1982, p. 136). All along, the patient has been projecting into the therapist the lively, active, split-off part of his self, while he remains inert and passive. The patient does not want, is not really concerned, and remains unambivalently paralyzed; in short, he is closer to the schizoid position.

HOW WOULD THE KLEINIAN MODEL UNDERSTAND A SUICIDE THREAT?

Once Ms. Yander, 32 years old, decided to let go of her last romantic relationship, depression surfaced fiercely and thoughts of suicide emerged. Her last boyfriend, while initially promising proved to be unreliable and disconnected from the patient's needs or affects. Ms. Yander was, however, a needy, greedy woman who angrily wanted a man to fill her up emotionally and financially.

In the session the patient emphasized that she was so depressed that she no longer wanted to live. She was through with crying. She had no boyfriend, her girlfriends were temporarily not available, her job was dreadful, and her family did not care enough about her. She had had it with creditors, who plagued her with calls.

I felt anxious and pressured, as if my hands were tied. Ms. Yander would not consider looking into herself to ascertain what she was doing to maintain her despair and sense of persecution. No possibility existed of any good being recognized or let in.

Faced with her massive projective identifications into me, I felt despair and frantic depression. I had thoughts of magically rescuing her, wishes for a new healthy man to come into her life who would be able to mother her and relieve her desperate neediness.

What flashed through my mind, both making me anxious and suggesting a strategy, was the idea of interpreting to her that she was maintaining the paranoid-schizoid position. She was doing this by not accepting responsibility for changing her life, her greediness, selecting immature men, and seeing the entire world as persecuting her in black-and-white terms, all of which resulted in not allowing any good in (e.g., from the fact that she had just received a raise). With regard to the raise, the patient spoiled that good by feeling it was not good enough. I worried about making all the preceding interpretations because I sensed that Ms. Yander would see me as being critical and persecuting. I believed that she had an impaired capacity to see me as a total person, that is, as a therapist who sympathized with her pain yet wanted to work on her paranoid-schizoid-position functions. She was for the moment not strongly enough present at the depressive position and thus able to be freer of her splitting and use of projective identification. I had to allow her to fill me with her projective identifications and, somehow, in the most gentle way, show her I felt compassion for her pain. I also had to help her acknowledge the need to look more totally at her own contributions to her plight.

WHAT IS AN EXAMPLE OF HOW TO REDUCE SPLITTING AND THE PATIENT'S SENSE OF HOPELESSNESS?

"I feel so bad, so hopeless. I just got some news that I must owe $3,000 to my former landlord. I'm just getting by as is. It's so unfair." All the preceding was said while Ms. Vincent, a divorced, 35-year-old secretary, dabbed at her eyes.

I knew the patient feared that ultimately she would be alone and helpless if she did not marry. Her conflict concerning marriage had been a constant theme in previous sessions. I said, "I guess you're feeling very alone and unlovable now."

"Yes, hopeless, but not as helpless."

When I heard that the patient did not feel helpless, I recognized that she was, despite her tears and verbalized despair, more at the depressive position. She could then use her internal objects to soothe herself, and the bad put into her by the landlord could be modified.

"Look," I said, "you were able to get through a difficult divorce, risk leaving an economically secure marriage and job for a better-paying job and it worked out. Also, you ended your relationship with your lover because that was not going anywhere, and that worked out, too." Here I was attempting to remind the patient that she had taken good care of herself in the past and reduce the split between her devalued, weak, hopeless self and her strong, capable self. She seemed able to soothe herself internally at this point, for she stated that she would consult a lawyer, and that she no longer felt so hopeless. The patient could come more in contact with the totality of her self (in the depressive position) and with lessened splitting and reexperiencing of that part of her self that was far from helpless. She was also more liberated from the despair of black-and-white convictions, which are so often a concomitant of the paranoid-schizoid position.

12

Treatment: From Start to Finish

When I first saw Mrs. Edelman five years ago, she had a masklike face excessively caked with rouge to disguise her depression and sense of deadness. I recall that I was momentarily taken aback by the severity of her striking, zombielike gait and affect.

Referred by another patient, Mrs. Edelman was desperately trying to escape her depression and find hope with another therapist. She had been in once-per-week psychotherapy with a psychiatrist for two years. For the past year he had given her large doses of antidepressant medication, and repeatedly tried to reassure her, despite her steadily increasing depression, that she would soon work through the sense of rejection and betrayal that had been inflicted on her by her lover.

I learned of the details of Mrs. Edelman's past history and current life over the course of several months. She apparently had a superb memory and could describe her childhood and current life in a vivid, compelling manner. There were many details, and sometimes I felt impatient as Mrs. Edelman piled detail upon detail as if she did not trust that I could truly understand her and what she had gone through and was going through now unless I knew every single fact. I processed her projections into me as a communication of her failure to be understood by the grownups in her childhood and what she was feeling about her husband's similar failure now. I also felt controlled by her obsessive narration and projection into me, of controlling objects in her life. She apparently had introjected them and was attempting to control me. I resolved to say something about this.

Mrs. Edelman has been married for thirty-five years to a man she portrays as chronically critical and devaluing of her. The patient had been strongly attracted to her husband when she first met him. He was exceptionally good-looking and superbly muscled. She thought herself the most fortunate of women to have captured what appeared to her initially as the most intelligent, talented, handsome man on the face of the earth. He was, at first, very attentive, knowledgeable, sophisticated, understanding, and doting. He painted a picture of an unfolding marriage that would be close, uplifting, and endlessly fascinating. The patient said that during the early years of their marriage, women would approach her husband and, despite her presence, would offer their names and phone numbers to him. She recalled how possessive and jealous she was then. She also remembered how her wise prophetic father, sensing intuitively that her husband-to-be had significant destructive character traits, had pronounced the night before the wedding, "I'm making you a funeral, not a wedding." Of course, the patient did not listen to him.

Once married, Mrs. Edelman discovered her husband to be a colossal "phony." To the outside world, he was sensitive, empathic, kind, soliticous, and understanding. Privately, with Mrs. Edelman, he was a perpetual tyrant. Almost nothing the patient could do was correct. He informed her, for instance, that she was a bad cook, a terrible housekeeper, a bad mother, too friendly, too much of a spender, too enthusiastic, too naive, like a "parrot" filled with clichés, and on and on and on. There was only one area where her husband grudgingly acknowledged that she had genuine talent, and that was in bed. He praised her body and her passion. He also insisted on adhering to a rigid sexual format. There was only one sexual position allowed. She had to face away from him as he entered her from the rear. His explanation for this rigid rule of coitus was that she was "too big" vaginally and his penis needed more friction. He also would never sexually approach her directly, but established a ritual consisting of one formula sentence that he uttered just before they went to bed: "Shall I take the phone off the hook?"

Her husband had no friends and did not want anyone visiting their home. He established himself as the undisputed cook, house cleaner, and shopper. He declared that he could do those things significantly better than she could. He would wrap a rag around his head and, wearing only the briefest of bikinis to display his muscular torso to the fullest advantage, would zealously go about the task of cleaning their home.

The apartment was his exclusive domain, and the patient had to ask his permission to go to the refrigerator for any snack. Each time she entered their apartment, she had to scrape her shoes under his vigilant eyes. Dirt was the enemy and the patient was, to her husband, the bringer of dirt.

Mrs. Edelman has one child, a married son with whom she has a frustrating relationship; it is not as close as she would like. When her son was a child, her husband was a rigid, devaluing, and competitive father. He would become angry, for example, when the son, at times, might receive a larger portion of food than he. He criticized his son's appearance and body. Evidently, the son had an ectomorphic body type in contrast to Mr. Edelman's body-builder physique. Mrs. Edelman would assert herself and argue protectively on behalf of their son. She made the point that she would really oppose her husband only during those moments when he verbally abused her son. Mrs. Edelman felt that her son ought to be deeply grateful to her for her protectiveness and efforts to give to him emotionally and culturally all those things denied him by his father. In effect, the patient felt her son "owed" her, and, certainly in alliance with her, he should hate his father. Instead, to Mrs. Edelman's chagrin and bewilderment, her son seemed to run after his father seeking his approval and, at times, accorded him greater respect than he offered to the patient.

Both of her parents had come to this country from Russia and Poland as young adults. Her mother had remained in Europe for a time with the patient's two brothers while her father established himself economically in America before sending for his family a few years later. Four years after her mother's arrival in America, the patient was born.

Her father, while having little formal education, was a highly educated man who, through self-instruction, could read and write Hebrew. He apparently had a fine wit, great charm, and a superb memory. He was able to quote aptly and freely from the Hebrew Bible and the Talmud, a Jewish book of wisdom and sage guidance. He was widely respected in the community and held numerous leadership positions in religious and social organizations.

The patient was quite proud of her father's intelligence and the wide respect accorded him by the community. There was, however, another side to him.

He showed disdain toward the patient's mother. At times, he was sharply contemptuous of her and would bitterly excoriate her for having "killed" their firstborn son. Apparently the mother had, according to him, not acted soon enough and their infant son had expired from a respiratory illness that was so common in Europe during those years. He had never forgiven her for this tragedy, though she waited on him "hand and foot," worked by his side in their store, and never complained of the long, physically taxing hours. He felt she was "stupid" and dull.

Mrs. Edelman's mother showed the patient no physical affection. She seemed totally absorbed in the mission of obtaining her husband's grudging approval. If the mother dispensed any affection, it was toward Mrs. Edelman's older brothers.

The patient remembered that her early childhood was spent largely alone and anxious in the apartment. Leaving a neighbor in charge of her, her parents would both go off to their store at the crack of dawn and return late in the evening six days a week. Her father would, from time to time, praise Mrs. Edelman's wit and intelligence, saying that she was brighter than her two brothers. It was quite clear to me that the patient deeply respected and loved her father and had joined him in his disdain for her mother.

Her older brothers, both married, apparently did not respect the patient. They had wanted her to end her marriage. When she repeatedly told them one "horror story" after another about her husband but did not end the marriage, they treated her with disdain and sarcasm.

In psychoanalytic therapy, the patient established an obvious communication pattern. She would quickly enter the room, impatient to begin talking. She would then briefly bemoan the fact that so much had happened in her life and how little time she had in the sessions to get to all she wanted to share with me. She then would launch into her husband's latest mistreatment of her and her failed attempts to reach him. She would next go to her painful yearning for her former lover. How could he have ended the relationship? She gave him wonderful sex and love. He was a man, a wonderful, inventive lover, unlike her husband. Subsequent sessions also disclosed that her lover had been cruelly chauvinistic and persistently exploitative of her. In reality, their relationship had been a narrow exploitation of her as a part-object.

I observed during the sessions that the patient seemed to be more concerned with telling me one story after another than with letting in any interpretation. I would say something and the patient would pause ever so slightly, then rush on as if I had not spoken.

I felt discounted, useless, impotent. I recognized that the patient was projecting into me those affects she had experienced as a child in relation to her own parents and with her husband. Her projective identifications were in search of communication and control, and in the service of ridding herself of toxic introjects. Recognizing that at this time she needed to reduce her persecutory anxiety, I could sustain my role as a container to her obsessiveness.

When I initially brought this pattern to her attention, she continued to talk as if she had not heard me. We traced this projective identification to her seeing me as if I was her mother and she, like her father, was not going to pay attention to me. Sometimes, she perceived me as herself while she was her husband, not paying attention to her. At other times, when she saw me as herself, I became her brothers or her lover ignoring her. All these transference resistances that had the theme of rejection were noted, repeatedly interpreted, and worked through. Mrs. Edelman began to realize that she was defending against drawing closer to me out of fear that I would reject her as her father had done to her mother.

I had to contain the anxiety and frustration that the patient projected into me as she at first provocatively ignored me. I could feel the anger and loneliness that she felt when ignored by her mother, father, husband, and other significant objects in her life. I could succeed in containing her anger and loneliness by feeling a rush of sympathy and compassion for her painful, long-term, emotional isolation.

To convey the flavor of Mrs. Edelman's inner world, the best indices, I believe, are examples of her dream life. I will first relate the dreams, then the associations, followed by my understanding and interpretations to the patient. These two dreams occurred during the middle phase of treatment, when I was still being confronted with the patient's use of denial and "story-telling" resistance.

The first dream I call the "freezer" dream. In the dream Mrs. Edelman sees her freezer has no food. It is empty but she is not upset. Her mother is present in a shadowy fashion in the background.

Her associations were as follows. The "freezer" referred to supplies. The patient went on to talk about how she was feeling depleted because of her stormy marriage. She then remembered that her mother had frozen her out. Like her mother, the patient was getting older with not too many years left to her life. Like her mother, her life was also being spoiled and depleted. She then remembered the title of a children's book, *Care Pierre*. Like her mother, the patient does not care enough about herself.

Mrs. Edelman's second dream, which I call the "telephone" dream, was as follows.

The patient is telling someone on the phone that she has to get money to give to her. A couple overhear the patient.

The female of the couple acts as a decoy. The man is ominous looking. They do not seem to understand that it is not Mrs. Edelman's money. The man has a mustache.

Her associations were as follows. Money meant her husband's pension. He had recently threatened to turn his pension totally over to their son in the event of his death rather than to the patient. Mrs. Edelman would like the whole financial conflict with her husband to go away. She was concerned that the stress of the conflict would deplete her energy, impairing her ability to work. She felt that the entire dream had a "cloak-and-dagger" atmosphere. The man in the dream reminded Mrs. Edelman of her father. He, too, had a mustache.

As I listened to her dreams, I associated to a very painful period in my own childhood when I would retreat to the roof of the apartment building where I lived to nurse in safety my resentments and grievances against my own parents. I had felt very much alone then, and had yearned for some adults who would understand me. I again felt a sadness and sympathy with the patient's sense of emotional isolation, a communicative projective identification that strengthened my containing function.

We can view the patient's dreams through the Kleinian lens as a graphic portrayal of her back-and-forth movement between the paranoid-schizoid and depressive positions. Mrs. Edelman's inner world was "frozen" and depleted by her mother's persecutory treatment of her infant and child self. The patient had been virtually ignored as a child and even physically abandoned by her mother, for example, left alone for an entire day in the apartment while the parents were at work. Like her mother, the patient had introjected little appropriate, adequate concern for herself. She had run after her rejecting husband like her mother had pursued her frustrating, disdainful, angry husband, the patient's father.

For a long time the patient had accepted the emptiness and meaninglessness of her marriage that had been fostered by her husband's tyrannical treatment of her.

Her second dream, the "telephone" dream, reveals more dramatically how Mrs. Edelman used the decoy resistance of tangential obsessiveness as a means of running away from a meaningful concern for herself and employing appropriate security measures. Because the patient did not feel she owned her own life—that is, the money in the dream was not really hers—she gave in too easily and diminished her own responsibility to take control over her own life.

I decided to speak to Mrs. Edelman about her "decoy" resistance depicted in the "telephone" dream. Since she appeared to be involved and curious about the meaning of her dream and seemed to be making a commitment to understanding it, I said to myself, "She must have projected into me a concerned piece of herself. I will give this healthy aspect of her back through an interpretation." I also reasoned that as long as the patient could maintain a dissociative mental state through distraction, interpretations of content were worthless, and she would continue to run away from the paranoid anxiety of her mother's abandonment of her and of her father's and husband's failure to rescue her from the frightful abyss of isolation. I also perceived myself as a transferential figure in the dream, the mustached man, who threatened her by expecting more from her than she believed she had to give, for example, "they do not seem to understand that it is not my money."

The patient's distractive technique of storytelling and obsessiveness, an introjection of her father's impressive, powerful, communicative capacity, was fighting off the depressive anxiety of possibly hurting her father and mother and me through concern for us all for not saving her from her painful childhood and current tormenting marriage and isolating abandonment. I repeatedly invited Mrs. Edelman, when she used her storytelling, obsessive maneuver, to consider why she was running away from specific dangers and anxieties. The patient's "decoy" resistance was deeply entrenched, and it took many sessions of repeated interpretations to finally allow her to develop enough trust me as a reliable, safe container of her persecutory and depressive anxieties, to give up what to her were vital protective distractions.

To handle the impoverishment of her marriage, the patient had developed an outside support group consisting of a married niece, co-workers, and a much older woman. The niece apparently served as a substitute daughter, respectful and admiring of the patient's competence and intelligence. Her co-workers were also, in part, transferential substitute daughters who compensated the patient for the lack of adequate endorsement from her husband, son, and brothers. The much older woman friend allowed the patient to make transferential reparations to her mother. The patient would cheer her friend up when she was frightened and depressed by frequent life-threatening illnesses. In turn, her friend, unlike the patient's mother, warmly praised Mrs. Edelman's intelligence and capacity for kindness and compassion.

As the patient's self-esteem rose, she began to challenge her husband's scornful tyranny and rigid needs. She also realized that her former lover was just another edition of her rejecting husband and brothers. It was at first extremely difficult for her to accept the notion that, in some respects, she had selected a man, her husband, who treated her the same way her father had treated her mother. The patient kept emphasizing that her father, unlike her husband, was a vital part of the community. However, in time, she sadly recognized that her father had indeed treated her mother unfairly and that he had subtly contributed to an oedipal rivalry between the patient and her mother. Mrs. Edelman was able to get in touch with some compassion for her mother. She also realized that telling her son and her brothers one marital horror story after another only made her look bad, like one who passively and masochistically accepted abuse. Once she stopped complaining to them, she began to notice that their respect for her increased.

Along with the increase of the patient's self-esteem, she developed a growing idealizing transference. I was remarkable. I had changed her life. She was so lucky that she had found me because she was near death when she first came to me. My insights into her, her husband, and her family were inevitably astute and valid, and so forth. I also noticed that she was wearing tighter skirts and, in general, dressing in a more sexually provocative manner. In one session during this phase of idealizing and erotic transferences, Mrs. Edelman declared that she could really satisfy a man. No matter how happy that man might be with his wife, he could not possibly have the kind of sexual experience she could provide. This was followed by a long, intense gaze. I interpreted that it was natural for her to be grateful to me for having gotten her through a difficult time and for working well with her in developing a better, more likable picture of herself, and obtaining greater insight into her husband and her family. I emphasized that there was more to her than her sexual desirability, and that I could be more helpful to her as her therapist than as her lover. I also commented that we could not have gotten as far as we had without her own strong desire to grow and her excellent capacity to integrate insights and act on them. This interpretation emphasized our therapeutic partnership and distributed responsibility between us for her gains that were momentarily diluted by the erotic transference.

The patient brought in a dream in the next session.

She was in her house and I was outside. I had a hose in my hand and was connecting it to her house.

The patient easily interpreted the dream, with a minimum of associations, to mean a wish for me to have sex with her. Now her bitter anger and envy surfaced. "Sure," she said, "it was easy for you to say you could be more helpful to me as a therapist instead of as a lover, because you have love in your life." According to her, I had a wife who was fortunate enough to have such an outstanding, sensitive man. What did she have? A freak! A misfit! A man who lived in a coffin and wanted her to crawl inside the coffin with him. Did my wife really appreciate me? Did she love me as much as Mrs. Edelman did? Could my wife give me as much as she could? Could she give me the kind of good sex that she knew she could give me?

All these questions exploded out of her. I asked her what her fantasies were about my marriage. She looked at me coyly and said, "I don't think you're happy. I don't think your sex life is good."

"Why?"

"Oh, I don't really know, but I do know it would be a lot better with me. I just have an intuitive knack for being a good sex partner. I really know how to satisfy a man."

And so it went. I repeatedly had to stress that there was more to her than her sexuality, that there might be a man out there other than me who would appreciate her totally: her sexual talents as well as her passion for life, capacity to care, and her intelligence. She never fully let go of the erotic transference, finally asserting that some day, so a neighborhood astrologer had informed her, I would become her spouse.

In the meantime, she met a man at work who showered her with compliments. He liked her sensuality but also her humor, intelligence, and perceptivity. She began to see him on weekends and they became lovers. During this termination phase of therapy, she brought in a dream that I shall relate, contrasting it with an earlier dream presented during the beginning phase of therapy.

Both the termination and beginning phase dreams have manifest contents that are almost transparently clear, needing little extension through free association.

The termination dream is as follows.

> The patient was being pursued by a group of men. She ran into a room filled with women. She still felt afraid and saw a narrow window. At first she hesitated to jump through the window to try to escape. She was on the thirteenth floor. She jumped through the window and landed safely on both feet.

The manifest content of the dream deals with a threat coming from men. She associated her husband to the group of men, since he comes on to her like an abusive gang. To women, she associated her mother, who was not an adequate model of appropriate self-caring and protection against an abusive man. The thirteenth floor produced the association of misfortune, her poor marriage, her bad luck. However, in the dream she risks and saves herself; she lands safely on both feet.

During the early phase of therapy, the patient had dreamt that she was in a small house in the woods. There was snow all around. She wanted to leave but she did not have any shoes.

The manifest content of this dream as well as her associations conveyed a sense of inadequacy, a feeling of being trapped in an intolerable, "cold" situation (her marriage) and her internal world.

I believe that the contrasting dynamics, as portrayed in the preceding two dreams originating from two different time periods in the therapy, vividly represent the progress the patient has made from an initial place of helplessness and entrapment to a point of vigorous, adaptive self-assertion.

As seen previously in the evocation of memories of my own painful feelings of childhood emotional isolation and of being misunderstood and discounted, the processing of my countertransferences was a key element for proper understanding of the patient's dynamics.

At first, I had responded to the patient's placing into me her hurt, persecuted self with an excessive need to rescue and repair her. The patient had evoked in me painful memories of my mother tearfully and piteously complaining to me when I was a child of my "weak" father's mistreatment of her — how trapped she felt. Then, as well as with the patient, I felt compelled to assume too much of the responsibility of rescuing her, too much concern with repairing her. When I recognized this disruptive countertransference stemming from my depressive position and the oedipal competition with my father, I could step back and offer more realistic, neutral analytic aid — a more appropriate distribution of responsibility and a more effective focusing, looking mainly at her own behavior. I could concentrate on what the patient was doing or not doing to foster her depression and sadomasochistic marriage.

I could also more clearly challenge her perception of her husband and her life in black-and-white terms. As Mrs. Edelman added more and more details to her understanding of her husband, it became clear that he was a very sick man, but the patient had selected him and did, at times, provoke him. More importantly, she was still choosing to remain in the marriage. It became increasingly clear that she needed her husband as a persecuting object, as a possible way of neutralizing her guilt for having oedipally triumphed over her mother and her brothers.

Although the patient appeared to be functioning mainly

in the depressive position—that is, she could relate to people totally, could tolerate ambivalence, and could be reflective and insightful—she was treating herself as a part-object. A piece of her self was always suffering or dead with her husband; another part of her self was very much alive outside of her marriage.

The main defense and massive resistance was a deep, underlying, powerful conviction that she really did not matter. What mattered was only herself as a highly desirable sexual part-object. When she could finally move from the paranoid-schizoid position of experiencing herself as only a part-object to the depressive position, more aware and concerned about herself totally, about her talents, her sensitivity, her passion for life, her compassion, and her capacity to give to others, she could challenge her husband's pathology and begin to extricate herself from what at first appeared to be a hopeless state.

The patient's central dynamic appeared to be the splitting off of the envious oedipal feelings and phantasies she had toward her mother for having her idealized father in a way she could not have and her envy toward her brothers for receiving her mother's affection. Since she could function at the depressive position, she could feel guilt and concern regarding her envy. She attempted to assuage her guilt by punishing herself through a terrible sadomasochistic marriage and obtaining gratification by marrying a man who appeared initially to be an idealized version of her father. Other women, maternal surrogates, would then, she believed, envy her. She had hoped that by symbiotically merging with her idealized husband, she could negate her part-object, paranoid-schizoid status, that is, her worth solely as a wonderful sexual partner, and ultimately migrate to a healthy level of concern for herself as a total object, in the depressive condition. Instead, her husband, as well as her lover and brothers, inflicted pain, only confirming for her her devalued, paralyzed state of despair.

Faced with guilt, poor self-esteem, and envy of other women who did have more gratifying total relationships with men, she used projective identification to place the needy aspects of herself into other men. This made it impossible for her to separate from them. She also used projective identification to evacuate the anxious, depressed parts of her self into me. That was why I initially experienced the patient as almost totally unable to take in and integrate any interpretations offered to her.

Her projective identifications were also communicative, and I could recognize, understand, interpret, and work through Mrs. Edelman's use of evacuation, which kept her feeling empty and greedy for more and more emotional sustenance in therapy. In this sense, she was emulating her greedy father and greedy husband, who were never satisfied with a woman's offerings. The patient had split off the greedy internal father object so that she could not readily undo the split. It was, of course, much easier for her to perceive the critical, devaluative behavior of her husband.

When Mrs. Edelman projected her evacuations into me, I gave her back as a good container concern, prizing of her worth, and non-anxiety. She could introject the good given back to her in the form of my interpretations and silent, empathic listening. I contained her insatiability by sensing compassionately the desperate cries in back of it, and she must have introjected me as a satisfactory introject in opposition to her greedy paternal introject.

Regarding her splitting, my projection back into her of that part of her self that was potent and alive reinforced the healthy, strong part of herself. As the patient in therapy undid the split between that part of her self that was almost dead and without power, and that part of her self present away from home that was alive and extremely potent, she took more responsibility for her life. She could become more assertive and could curb her need to sabotage her self-esteem through compulsive masochistic experiences.

She was able to gain increased respect from her brothers and obtain challenging employment, healthy friends, and nourishing intimacy. Diminished evacuative projective identification permitted the patient to tap more fully into her understanding, sensitivity, and capacity for compassion. She could now listen more and offer a vastly improved, more effective empathic response.

A postscript: During the last year of the termination phase, with much embarrassment, reluctance, and hesitation, Mrs. Edelman finally revealed a "secret," one that she had kept from me, feeling that I would censure her, find her "sick," disgusting, or "crazy." I should add parenthetically, as I have done before, that the two greatest underlying anxieties patients in general bring into therapy are the fear that they will be driven crazy by the therapist (a paranoid-schizoid anxiety) or that they will drive the therapist crazy (a depressive anxiety). The patient had apparently found me to be a good enough container, strong enough to weather her turmoil and caring enough not to attack her, that she could challenge these two anxieties, and so she shared her "dreadful, dirty" secret with me.

When Mrs. Edelman shared this secret with me, I experienced a number of feelings. I was touched that she trusted me enough to challenge her paternal and spousal introjects that showered her with self-disgust and self-deprecation. I admired her courage and her growth. I felt a momentary sense of gratitude toward her for validating me as an appropriate reparative container characterized by safety, reliability, and understanding. At the same time, I remembered my own shameful, "dirty" secret that had so terribly injured me emotionally in fourth grade. I had been left back because I had not passed arithmetic. Painful as this trauma was, even more painful was my parents' attitude toward my suffering. In their view I had brought them embarrassment and dishonor. I was instructed to tell no one. Instead, I was to lie and hope that no neighborhood *yenta* (busybody) would discover my hideous, shameful secret. I tried desperately to carry out their injunction and to conceal what was so clear to me then, that is, the obvious stigma of my intellectual defectiveness. The patient's projections into me of her "terrible" secret resonated with my own past self-disgust, worry over possible discovery of my secret, and sense of abandonment by my parents.

I also remembered that during fourth grade, my maternal grandmother had lived within walking distance. I would frequently visit her alone and tell her of my anguish. She would listen patiently, offer me a glass of tea with a peeled slice of apple floating in it (Russian style) and a cube of sugar and tell me with absolute conviction that my parents were *meshuga* (crazy) for burdening me with a "secret" and being indifferent to my anguish. She was a superb container — soothing, reliable, and understanding. Unlike my parents, she had her priorities straight. I realized similarly that all along I had been introjecting Mrs. Edelman's shame, self-disgust, and self-hate and had projected good back into her, saying such things as, "You reached out for love, not merely sex. You did not want to be merely a tool for your husband's self-centered sex." My telling the patient this served to further her movement from her paranoid-schizoid position of viewing herself disparagingly and basically as a useless part-object only, to the depressive-position view of herself as a total object whose feeling, thinking, and doing really mattered. And she had the right to seek love, intimacy, and understanding, qualities absent in her childhood home and her marriage. With her own greater depressive-position perspective as a complicated, struggling human being who was not to be judged by herself in black-and-white terms, she could then be kinder to herself just as I, as a traumatized fourth-grader, could be kinder and effectively repairing to myself when contained within the accepting, integrating crucible of my grandmother's concerned recognition of my total personhood.

And now the secret. It seems that Mrs. Edelman's husband had urged her to have sex with another man. It turned him on. He had even selected her lover as a likely prospect.

The patient had to agree to tell him every detail of the sexual encounter, had to consent to his listening to her telephone conversations with her lover, and had to go along with not douching herself after sex with her lover, so that Mr. Edelman could later lick the sperm. Most important, Mr. Edelman decreed that the patient was not to hide anything from him and not to fall in love with her lover. The patient had, unbeknownst to her husband, violated this last commandment. After sharing her "secret" with me and experiencing my understanding, continued respect, and acceptance of her, she felt "clean," free to go on with her life.

She left her husband and is now living with the man she met at her office. Our final session was warmly emotional. She had begun therapy as a walking "corpse," a willing "caged" bird. She was leaving therapy alive, able to live life without the severe masochistic constraints imposed by her sadistic, tyrannical husband, a split-off, persecuting aspect of her self.

A year after she ended treatment, I received a brief note.

Dear Dr. Solomon,

Everything is going well. Thanks for my life! Thanks for helping me to grow, to risk, to endure pain and survive, to feel free, and ultimately to to have fun again (smile).

Warmly,

Mrs. Edelman

Epilogue

The many vignettes in this book demonstrate clearly the value of the Kleinian model in furthering our clinical understanding and technical skills. The concepts of introjection and projective identification render the boundary between the therapist and the patient porous and fluid, allowing the therapist to have a more sensitive awareness of his own and the patient's internal worlds. Postulating constant introjection and projective identification, the Kleinian therapist can register more delicately the patient's anxieties, guilt, defenses, idealizations, introjects, and, in general, the content of the patient's phantasies. This leads to an increased humility and recognition that psychotic-like organizations always exist within us, differing only in degree and resolution for each of us.

During the fast-moving pace of once- or twice-per-week therapy, Kleinian theory generates useful clinical hypotheses, as follows.

Idealization may be followed by devaluating envy. Bad or good introjects may be projected into the therapist as a form of communication, control, or safekeeping. Good introjects may be projected into an object, and anxiety about depletion of the good by the object may follow. Any feeling or fantasy the therapist has may be a directive toward a possible defense against an introject that is projected into him by the patient. What the therapist is most anxious about saying to the patient may very well be what needs to be said. Persecutory and guilty anxieties may often be associated with part-object introjections and projective identifications. Clarification of splitting and repeated interpretations may lead to integration, an aspect of the depressive position, or warding off disintegration, a feature of the paranoid-schizoid position.

Every therapist has encountered impasses, a therapeutic paralysis characterized by repetitive, stale sessions caused by subtle resistances, transferences, or countertransferences. The Kleinian model is particularly well suited to understanding and unclogging impasses, because it emphasizes the fluid, back-and-forth transmission between therapist and patient of introjects, defenses, anxieties, and phantasies. The whole dyadic therapy field is scrutinized. Melanie Klein's pioneering delineation of envy is also essential in battling impasses and the special impasse known as the Negative Therapeutic Reaction (NTR).

Greater awareness of the borderline and the narcissistic patient supports Kleinian insights. Embodying many aspects of the paranoid-schizoid and depressive positions, both the narcissistic and the borderline patient may treat significant objects in their lives as part-objects. There may also be an

absence of concern and/or a rapid fluctuation between guilt ✓ ʃρ
and a sense of being persecuted.

Melanie Klein's contributions, like Freud's, narrowed
the supposed gap of pathology between the patient and the
therapist, so much so that many mental health professionals
could not accept her theory and technical suggestions. Apparently, Klein's idea that psychotic functioning occurs from
birth on and is organized in discernible constellations
sounded too irrational and fantastic to them. They forgot
that Freud's fundamental discoveries sat on the basic finding
that the irrational exists and determines every aspect of our
mental functioning, as fantastic as that initially may sound.
Freud demonstrated further that the irrational had definite
patterns. Klein has significantly extended our understanding ₂
of Freud's magnificent rediscovery of the childishly irrational
by adding the infantile irrational. To properly understand
and effectively work with and reach our patients, both
irrationalities, Klein's infantile and Freud's childish, need to
be taken into account.

Suggested Reading

Melanie Klein's ideas are not systematically developed in textbook fashion. Rather, they are scattered throughout her papers and books. Her work, I think, can be optimally approached by first absorbing clarifying organized expositions of her ideas, for example, Segal and Weininger. Her followers Bion, Rosenfeld, Joseph, and Meltzer have added their own observations to her basic theory, clinical contributions, and technique.

Hanna Segal (1964). *An Introduction to the Work of Melanie Klein*. London: Heinemann. 2nd ed, London: Hogarth, 1973.

It is best to begin with this book, since it is a clear explanation of Klein's basic theoretical concepts. Dr. Segal offers interesting and illustrative clinical vignettes taken from her psychoanalytic practice.

Hanna Segal (1981). *The Work of Hanna Segal*. New York: Jason Aronson.

 Almost all of Dr. Segal's published papers are contained here. She discusses, among many diverse clinical issues, the curative elements in psychoanalysis, dreams, artistic creativity, and schizophrenia.

O. Weininger (1984). *The Clinical Psychology of Melanie Klein*. Springfield, IL: Charles C Thomas.

 A brief, clear exposition of Klein's ideas, fundamental to the understanding of child and adult behavior.

Melanie Klein (1975). *The Writings of Melanie Klein*. Vols. 1–4. London: Hogarth.

 These are four volumes that contain Melanie Klein's books and papers, ranging from her first paper, written in 1926, to her last book, published in 1961. I consider the following her most seminal contributions to theory and technique:

 A Contribution to the Psychogenesis of Manic-Depressive States (1935)

 Mourning and the Relation to Manic-Depressive States (1940)

 Notes on Some Schizoid Mechanisms (1946)

 The Origin of Transference (1952)

 A Study of Envy and Gratitude (1957)

 A Narrative of a Child Analysis (1961)

Robin Anderson, ed. (1992). *Clinical Lectures on Klein and Bion*. London/New York: Tavistock/Routledge.

 A collection of papers by Kleinian analysts originally presented to a lay audience to introduce them to the ideas of Klein and Bion. The papers give an excellent account of contemporary Kleinian analysis, influenced by Bion's contributions.

Herbert Rosenfeld (1987). *Impasse and Interpretation*. London: Tavistock.

The last work of a pioneer who bravely treated psychotics from a Kleinian perspective. He deals with therapeutic and antitherapeutic elements, narcissism, projective identification, countertransference, and changing theories and techniques.

Betty Joseph (1989). *Psychic Equilibrium and Psychic Change: Selected Papers of Betty Joseph.* Edited by E. B. Spillius and M. Feldman. London: Routledge.

Betty Joseph informs us about the psychopathic personality, the patient who is difficult to reach, different types of anxiety, passivity, envy, projective identification, and other major clinical concerns. She accompanies all her observations with exquisitely astute, detailed clinical vignettes.

Wilfred Bion (1977). *Seven Servants: Four Works by Wilfred Bion.* New York: Jason Aronson.

Perhaps the most brilliant follower of Melanie Klein, Bion is evocative and creative. He has a way of coming at the reader from unexpected directions and pushing him to challenge clinical assumptions. He is also difficult to read, for his ideas are closely packed and abstract. He strives for almost algebraic formulations and interrelationships. He was able to enter the world of the psychotic and gather conceptual observations that apply usefully to every other aspect of behavior (e.g., container/contained).

James S. Grotstein, ed. (1983). *Do I Dare Disturb the Universe?: A Memorial to Wilfred R. Bion.* London: H. Karnac.

The contributors to this work reflect the profound stimulation Bion has given many analysts. The volume includes an absorbing account by Dr. Grotstein of Bion, the man, and his work.

Donald Meltzer (1967). *The Psycho-Analytical Process.* London: Heinemann.

Donald Meltzer (1978). *The Kleinian Development.* Vols. 1–3. Perthshire: Clunie.

In the above books, Dr. Meltzer applies Klein's concepts to child and adult analysis. He also examines the clinical development of Freud, Klein, and Bion. Volume 3 details and critiques Klein's last major work, *The Narrative of a Child Analysis* (1961).

I. Saltzberger-Wittenberg (1970). *Psycho-Analytic Insights and Relations: A Kleinian Approach.* London: Routledge and Kegan Paul.

   Written for social workers, Dr. Saltzberger-Wittenberg's book very nicely illustrates how Kleinian concepts can be applied to various challenging clinical situations and crises.

Phyllis Grosskurth (1986). *Melanie Klein: Her World and her Work.* New York: Knopf.

   As the book's title implies, Dr. Grosskurth provides information concerning Melanie Klein's professional contributions and her personal life. The author conveys with great skill Klein's brave determination to offer to psychoanalysis her valuable clinical and theoretical insights, despite fierce opposition from powerful colleagues.

R. D. Hinshelwood (1989). *A Dictionary of Kleinian Thought*: London: Free Association Books.

   A superb, comprehensive reference presenting and illuminating Kleinian and post-Kleinian concepts.

References

Amiel, H. F. (1975). In *Quotations of Wit and Wisdom*, ed. J. W. Gardner and F. G. Reese, p. 78. New York: Norton.

Bion, W. (1957). Differentiation of the psychotic from the non-psychotic personalities. *International Journal of Psycho-Analysis* 38:266-275.

———— (1959). Attacks on linking. *International Journal of Psycho-Analysis* 40:308-315.

———— (1962). *Learning from Experience*. London: Heinemann.

Grosskurth, P. (1986). *Melanie Klein: Her World and Her Work*. New York: Knopf.

Jacobs, T. (1993). The inner experiences of the analyst: their contribution to the analytic process. *International Journal of Psycho-Analysis* 74:7-14.

Joseph, B. (1959). An aspect of the repetition compulsion. *International Journal of Psycho-Analysis* 40:1-10.

———— (1960). Some characteristics of the psychopathic personality. *International Journal of Psycho-Analysis* 41:526-531.

———— (1978). Different types of anxiety and their handling in the analytic situation. *International Journal of Psycho-Analysis* 59:223–228.

———— (1982). Addiction to near-death. *International Journal of Psycho-Analysis* 63:449–456.

———— (1983). On understanding and not understanding: some technical issues. *International Journal of Psycho-Analysis* 64:291–298.

———— (1989). *Psychic Equilibrium and Psychic Change.* New York/London: Tavistock/Routledge.

Klein, M. (1927). Symposium on child analysis. In *The Writings of Melanie Klein*, vol. I, pp. 139–169. London: Hogarth, 1975.

———— (1932). *The Psychoanalysis of Children.* In *The Writings of Melanie Klein*, vol. II, pp. 3–326. London: Hogarth, 1975.

———— (1937). *Love, Guilt, and Reparation.* In *The Writings of Melanie Klein,* vol. I, pp. 306–343. London: Hogarth, 1975.

———— (1946). Notes on some schizoid mechanisms. In *The Writings of Melanie Klein*, vol. III, pp. 1–24. London: Hogarth, 1975.

———— (1950). On the criteria for the termination of a psychoanalysis. In *The Writings of Melanie Klein*, vol. III: pp. 43–56. London: Hogarth, 1975.

———— (1952a). Some theoretical conclusions regarding the emotional life of infants. In *The Writings of Melanie Klein*, vol. III, pp. 61–93. London: Hogarth, 1975.

———— (1952b). The origins of transference. In *The Writings of Melanie Klein*, vol. III, pp. 48–56. London: Hogarth, 1975.

———— (1957). *Envy and Gratitude.* In *The Writings of Melanie Klein*, vol. III, pp. 176–235. London: Hogarth, 1975.

———— (1961). *A Narrative of a Child Analysis.* In *The Writings of Melanie Klein*, vol. IV, pp. 11–496. London: Hogarth, 1975.

Lindbergh, A. M. (1955). *Gift from the Sea.* New York: Pantheon.

Money-Kyrle, R. (1956). Normal countertransference and some of its deviations. *International Journal of Psycho-Analysis* 37:360–366.

Racker, H. (1974). *Transference and Countertransference.* New York: International Universities Press.

Rosenfeld, H. (1971). Contribution to the psychopathology of psychotic states: the importance of projective identification in the ego structure and object relations of the psychotic patient. In *Impasse and Interpretation.* London: Tavistock, 1987.

———— (1987). *Impasse and Interpretation.* London: Tavistock.

Index